BLUE LIGHTS

[1]

BLUE LIGHTS IN MY REARVIEW

BY

RICHARD TAYLOR

ISBN: **978-0-9970227-6-6**

Taylor House Publishing
405 Olivia Lane
Goldsboro, NC 27530
(919) 587-7782

taylorpublishinghouse@gmail.com
www.facebook.com/taylorhousepublishing

Printed by:
Precision Printing
1300 Priority Lane
Chesapeake, VA 23324

Graphic Design: Taylor House Publishing

Dedication

This book is dedicated to every male of African descent in the United States of America who has had any contact with the criminal justice system. This is for every black man who has been stopped unjustly, illegally searched, racially profiled, unlawfully detained, police brutalized, falsely arrested, mistreated, disrespected and criminalized by law enforcement officers. This is for those who have been wrongfully convicted, poorly represented, over-prosecuted, over-sentenced, unfairly tried, and coerced into plea agreements by America's judicial system. Most importantly, this work is a tribute to those lives that were unworthy of death but died by the overzealous actions of police officers in their role to serve and protect. While there are too many to list, this book is a tribute to their lives, the legacy of their families and the memories of the tragic, senseless, unnecessary manner which their lives ended prematurely. May God bless us all; as we endure and overcome the injustices, oppression, discrimination, prejudice, and outright racism that have plagued this country for centuries. Peace, Love, and Blessings to all.

Table of Contents

Preface

In the United States today there is an uprising. The year 2020 has birthed an awakening to the long ignored elephant in the room. This animal has existed unaddressed to the point that it has overgrown the small corner it was previously hidden. It has now fully matured to the extent that it has outgrown the entire house and spills out into the front yard and streets.

Windows are being broken, fires are being ignited, the water mains are being ruptured and buildings are being destroyed. Occupants of the house and neighbors are realizing what many have known and refused to acknowledge for quite some time. Something must be done about this damned elephant!!

The allegorical animal that I refer to is the blatant, systematic brutalization, dehumanization, criminalization and the outright murder of African males in the United States by police officers. The residents of this symbolic house are the judges, police captains, prosecutors, legislators, politicians, power brokers and everyday citizens who have routinely turned a blind eye, excused, justified and even contributed to the growth and development of this savage beast.

The windows, fires and destruction I refer to is the literal rioting and unrest that has engulfed many cities across this country. It also includes the shaking of the foundational policies and practices of every institution from schools, religion, politics, laws, economics, healthcare, military, entertainment and anything else that influences American culture.

Lastly, the neighbors are other countries looking from the outside in, noticing the mistreatment of certain people and wondering why the animal has been allowed to grow. They are beginning to stand with the victims in solidarity against the owners of the ill-conditioned house. They too are demanding that the elephant be slaughtered.

These neighbors are wondering how this treatment has continued unchecked for so long. They wonder, what is the basis for this dislike, and when did it start. They wonder, how can the victims, keep enduring the treatment without retaliation? They contemplate, how will it end?

Despite the outside scrutiny, or the desperate cries of the occupants, the owners of the house have longed denied the problem. The provocateurs, participants and the privileged members of the racist systems that allow these actions have accepted them as a necessary evil. They consider it as collateral damage of the great edifice they have built. They justify it with all types of sociopolitical and philosophical jargon, much to the chagrin of people who know and have experienced the truth.

Many of the victimized occupants of the house have also grown disillusioned. They embrace and justify their condition as a normal part of life. Some contribute to the stereotypes; committing actions that warrant the validation of said treatment. Many even go as far as to teach their children to expect to be treated different; psychologically castrating them before they even reach mental puberty.

However, there are those on all three sides of the spectrum that refuse to allow this monster to live. They have begun to uproot, upset, and upheave institutions and thought patterns that are not conducive to the equal treatment of all humanity. They have begun to express ideas, share experiences and initiate conversation that can lead to the end of such evil practices.

I am one of those persons. I refuse to allow something as horrible, torrid, and horrendous as racism to exist without doing my part to fight it. So, I write these words; in order expose the soft white underbelly of America that far too many have experienced, but few have the gall to speak about or the words to articulate. I feel like this is my duty, my right as laid forth in America's own Declaration of Independence. The words of Thomas Jefferson still echo in my mind as I think about the condition of black men in America today.

"We hold the truths to be self-evident, that all men are created equal, that they are endowed by the Creator with certain inalienable Rights, that among these are Life, Liberty and the pursuit of Happiness.- That to secure these rights, Governments are instituted among Men, deriving their just powers from the consent of the governed.-That whenever any Form of Government becomes destructive of these ends, it is the Right of the people to alter or abolish it, and institute a new Government, laying its foundation on such principles and organizing its powers in such form, as to them shall seem most likely to affect their Safety and Happiness...."

Thomas Jefferson
Declaration of Independence
August 2, 1976

Isaiah 10:1, 2 "Woe to those who make unjust laws, to those who issue oppressive decrees to deprive the poor of their rights and withhold justice from the oppressed of my people..."

Introduction

I remember like it was yesterday. I may have been nine or ten years old. It was a regular Saturday morning for me and my sisters. Chores in the morning were followed by a little recreation, before having to be at youth choir rehearsal at twelve o'clock.

From Taylor Street, our residence, to our church, was only a five minute drive. My mom rounded up my sisters and me and set out on the short trip to the church. This morning would be different than the rest, and change my perception of the world.

We arrived at the church early and noticed everyone standing outside instead of inside the sanctuary. Apparently, the deacon that normally let everyone in was absent and the doors were locked.

My father was superintendent of Sunday school and usually the first to arrive on Sundays. My mother knew he had a set of keys at home. I, my mother and another friend rushed from the church back to our house to retrieve the keys.

On the way back my mother drove down Harris Street faster than normal. Harris Street eventually turned into Bunche Drive, which led to John Street where the church stood. On Bunche was a hill sloping downward. At the top of the hill sat a police car on an intersecting street, as my mother passed.

Neither I, nor my mother saw the law enforcement officer. It was not until we reached the end of Bunche Drive, a block away from our destination, did we notice the blue lights flashing in the rearview mirror. My mother pulled over immediately. Exasperation, worry and scorn filled her now rattled demeanor.

"Oh shoot," she exclaimed while we waited for the officer to approach. "What, was I speeding? I know I wasn't going that fast! I hope I don't get a ticket," she pleaded out loud to no one in particular.

"Ma'am, let me see your license and registration," the white policeman commanded as he reached the window.

"Alright, I have it right here. Just give me a second," my mother stated while searching nervously for her purse. Then, she reached inside the glove compartment and handed both documents to the officer.

"Well, the reason why I stopped you is because I clocked you doing thirty-seven miles per hour coming down the hill. The speed limit is only twenty-five here. Where are you in such a rush to?"

"I'm sorry sir. I didn't know I was going that fast. I was just trying to get back to my church and let the children in. I had to go get the keys from my house because someone didn't show up. I was rushing because we are supposed to start at twelve o'clock sharp and it's almost that time now!"

"Okay, Mrs. Taylor, just hold up here for a minute. I'll be back shortly," the man responded coldly with no regard for my mother's explanation.

I waited in uncomfortable silence as the officer returned to his cruiser. My mother, now visibly distraught, voiced her concern over the possibility of receiving a ticket, as well as being late to open the church. I sat helplessly listening to her plead her case to the absent official.

"I haven't had a ticket in years! I was just trying to get back to the church on time. He was just sitting there parked, waiting on someone. Why did he have to stop me?"

The police officer reemerged with yellow and pink slips of paper. He informed my mother she would be charged with going 34 miles per hour in a 25 mile per hour zone. Shaking her head, my mother signed both papers and took her copy. I sensed her holding back tears all the while during the 30 second ride to the church.

Choir rehearsal was usually a jovial occasion. This day, it was a bit more somber as I thought of the prior situation. How could a police officer cause so much stress and strain on my pure, loving, caring and kind mother? Why couldn't he show her leniency under the circumstances? I mean, it wasn't like she was a hardened criminal. This was the first time that I felt disdain or contempt for police officials in my young life, but it would certainly not be the last.

While doing the research for the previous incident, I asked my mother was that the only time she ever got a ticket. In response, she said that there was one other instance before that, involving similar conditions.

While traveling on the same Harris Street, she came to a stoplight on the corner of Slocumb Street. She then made a right and headed North on Slocumb toward Ash Street. When she made a right turn on Mulberry, she was pulled over by a police officer. He stated the reason as her failure to completely stop at the light on Slocumb a mile back.

My mother's question about the incident today has echoed many others' sentiments over the years. Why did you wait so long to stop me? Why didn't you stop me when I first made the infraction? I would ask the same question of officers, years later on that same street.

In my years of experiences, my questions have gotten a lot deeper. Why did you stop me in the first place? Why did you turn your vehicle around when you saw me? Why did you run my license tags if I didn't do anything wrong? What did I do to make you follow me for all this time?

In the small town of Goldsboro, North Carolina, where I was raised, occurrences like these are all too common. There have always seemed to be a deep-rooted tension between the police and the black residents.

In a town where the population is roughly fifty percent black and fifty percent white, there is a disparity in the racial diversity of law enforcement. There are only twenty percent black officers in this city. The majority white police force must patrol a majority black neighborhood; people they don't know, have no connection to, and in most cases, don't understand. This is a recipe for disaster.

This situation is not only reserved for Goldsboro, NC. This problem exists across the United States. From Small Town, USA to big cities like Los Angeles, New York, Miami, and Chicago, law enforcement normally police communities they don't live in and rarely visit. This is one reason for the all too frequent ill-fated interactions between police and citizens.

On the receiving end of these encounters is the black man. Since the inception of police forces, we have always been their target. As a youth, I constantly heard that one in three black men will end up in jail. Today, there are more black men entangled in the legal system, than there are in college and that were enslaved at the end of slavery. Most staggeringly, black men are nearly three times more likely to killed, by law enforcement than their white counterparts.

Throughout history, one can follow the trail of this complex relationship between black men and the long arm of the law. With the abolition of slavery, the slave codes were instituted after the thirteenth amendment was passed. This allowed for slavery to continue if a person was convicted of a crime. It was then that black men were targeted by police for all sort of offenses and given large prison sentences, providing free labor on chain gangs.

Enter the Jim Crow and segregation eras where black men were again targeted, marginalized, dehumanized and criminalized by the laws and law enforcers of the land. The Ku Klux Klan, which was nothing but police, judges, senators, prosecutors, and sheriffs in disguise, carried out state sponsored terrorism on black men and their communities nationwide.

Fast forward to the civil rights and the Black Power time periods, where Federal Agents targeted leaders and organizations for "neutralization;" a code word for murder. Positive leaders like Martin King, Malcolm X, Medgar Evers, Huey Newton, Eldridge Cleaver, Fred Hampton, Geronimo Pratt, Mumia Abu Jamal and many others were targeted by the F.B.I.'s COINTELPRO agenda. Some were outright murdered by the state, and others were set up by police on trumped up charges. Many remain locked up as political prisoners or exiled as political refugees to this day.

The targeting continued into the 70's, 80's and 90's with reports of police brutality in black communities across the nation. This phenomenon was highlighted by the 1991 videotaped beating of Los Angeles resident Rodney King by six L.A. Police officers. The trial and subsequent acquittal of the officers sparked days of rioting that rival those of the 1960's and the recent upheavals of the present.

However, the incidences of police misconduct in 2020 are nothing new. In 1997, a Haitian immigrant, Abner Louima was arrested and sodomized with a plunger at the station by NYPD. In 1999, another immigrant, Amadou Diallo, died by 41 bullets from NYPD after reaching for his wallet. Sean Bell was the victim a 50-bullet barrage from NYPD while leaving his bachelor party in 2006. He died one day before his wedding.

These are just three instances of thousands that happened in the modern era. With the advent of social media within the last ten years, the knowledge and exposure of these occurrences have become widespread. Victims of police brutality, misconduct, negligence and homicide have become household names.

Trayvon Martin, Michael Brown, Tamir Rice, Eric Garner, Walter Scott, Alton Sterling,

Sandra Bland, Freddy Gray, Philando Castile, Stephon Clark, and many others have become synonymous with everything wrong with policing in America. Phrases like "Hands up, don't shoot," "I can't breathe," and "Say her name," memorialize these victims and keep the ferocity of their deaths ever-present in the public eye.

Because of this exposure, there is a fresh scrutiny of police practices, especially in communities of color. With the most recent, appalling deaths of Breonna Taylor, Rashard Brooks and the eight minute and forty-six second grueling recorded death of George Floyd from a police officer kneeling on his neck, outrage is at an all-time high. The subsequent riots have everyone, including police on high alert.

Today, there are many different dialogues regarding police reform and racism. There are people from all walks of life, taking their positions on various sides of the argument. Opinions contrast, emotions flare, and tensions rise as everyone feels their voice should be heard.

Some highlight the problem. Some offer solutions. Some share their experiences, insight and beliefs. Many ask the questions who, what, when where, why and how. Some justify, some excuse, some condemn, some condone, some jest and some ridicule the current state of police and black people in this country. This book will attempt to bring clarity to a situation that very few people have experienced or studied, and so very few understand.

Starting with the origin of policing in America, black men have always been the target of unfair and unjust treatment by the state via the police and judicial system. There are different phases in history where this treatment has continued in various shapes, forms and fashions at multiple levels of severity.

This book will examine past and present day cases, in which police brutality against people of color have gone unpunished. This will include the high-profile instances and little-known occurrences, including my own experiences with rogue police actions.

Additionally, I will discuss the complicity of other aspects of American society in the perpetuation of opinions, stereotypes, beliefs, and conditions that causes and excuses these acts of violence against blacks. Finally, I will explain the reasons these things continue to exist and what must be done on both sides of the issue to bring this senselessness to a halt.

Parts of this information may be unbelievable to some. The assertions may be offensive to others. Commentary could be considered one-sided. My experiences may be all too familiar to many.

No matter the viewpoint one has on these issues, the conversations will always be uncomfortable. These dialogues are necessary to bring understanding, closure, and solutions to this problem we all face today. Just think. If the mere discussion of this issue makes you uneasy, imagine how a man of African descent feels when he sees BLUE LIGHTS IN THE REARVIEW.

Chapter 1

The Origins of Police in America

In order to understand the current situation in, one must revert to the beginning of America. Many don't like to discuss this era of history because it exposes the savagery, brutality, and outright racism this country was founded upon. However, without understanding the mindset of the founders and their attitudes towards people of color, we will not come to the knowledge of the perceptions that exist today.

Starting on or about the year 1619, blacks who arrived in America were immediately placed in slavery. This relegated them to the property of white slave owners; no more than a beast or farm animal. Thus, they were treated as such.

During this time period, black men and women were worked without pay, beaten, raped, maimed, tortured, castrated, and even killed at the master's whim. There were no consequences for the inhumane treatment of blacks, or slaves as they were called. The victims suffered for decades with no advocate.

These conditions were considered normal, and even worse, legal. The slave masters were upstanding, law-abiding, Christians who practiced this evil. Judges, lawyers, sheriffs, mayors, senators, governors and even presidents reveled in the ownership of their fellow man. The dehumanization of Africans was completely sanctioned by the state.

Just imagine how the slaves felt. These were once proud kings and queens, tribal chiefs, princesses, and warriors who formally ruled, provided for and protected their own kingdoms, land and families. Now, they were stripped of their language, heritage, culture, legacy and humanity only to be treated worse than cattle of the field.

It was hard for the Africans to adapt to their captivity. It was difficult to speak the new language. It was no doubt awkward not having the normal, divine God-given control over one's body and destiny. Operating in this new environment made them slow, unsure, fearful, and dependent on their controllers.

The white slave masters used their discombobulation to justify the slave's predicament. They taught their children that blacks were stupid, incapable, savage, and cursed by God to be servants. Some even used the Holy Bible as a tool to further promote the enslavement of blacks.

However, within the human nature, there is an innate desire to be free. The uprisings of slaves like Nat Turner and Denmark Vesey, or the bravery of Harriett Tubman and Frederick Douglass escaping from slavery are very familiar. However, captives had been revolting and running away since the inception of slavery. Hence, the first form of oppressive policing towards blacks in America originated.

In the early 1700's the slave patrols were formed. These consisted of white land and slave owners who employed their peers. Their job was to quell slave rebellions, prevent escape, and capture courageous blacks who dared to defect from the treachery of plantation life. Some may say the first police force was erected to deliberately deny black people freedom in a so-called free society.

This attitude of white men towards blacks persisted unabated for the next couple of centuries. Even when the settlers were fighting for their independence from Britain, black men and women were denied freedom. Despite being drafted to assist in the war efforts, slave owners refused to keep their promise of liberty to those souls who risked their lives.

The great founding fathers' disdain for their African counterparts was evidenced in the foundational documents establishing this country's sovereignty. The hypocrisy of their ideology is laughable at best. In 1776 the Declaration of Independence stated that "all men are created equal." However, just a decade later, the Constitution that instituted the U.S. Government declared that blacks were only equaled to three-fifths of a person. Statutes like these allowed the unsavory treatment to continue, even after the country's liberation.

However, at the turn of the century, the nation's leaders and slave owners begin to feel the perils and dangers of their actions. In addition to keeping their slaves in line a situation brewing on a small island foreshadowed the inevitable. No doubt, the slave masters of the colonies took notice.

From 1791 to 1804 Toussaint Louverture and his Haitian Army led a successful revolution against the French colonist. As a result of his valiant efforts, the French were ousted from the island and Haiti earned its independence. This violent bloody war and the subsequent victory of blacks served as a precursor of things to come in the English colonies and a warning to slave owners.

As mentioned before, there were many uprisings of blacks during the period of slavery. None, however, is more renown than that of Nat Turner. In 1831 the seeds sown from the slave masters' brutality reaped the harvest of death upon their own heads.

In a two-day period in August of that year, Turner and his other "fugitive" slaves killed around 60 people in Southampton, VA. The county soon regrouped, gathered the cavalry and captured Nat Turner and his crew. The leader and his companions were speedily tried and hanged for their pursuit of freedom.

A few years earlier in South Carolina, Denmark Vesey was tried and hanged for the crime of planning a slave revolt. These are just two examples of the state criminalizing black men for attempting to exercise the God given rights of life, liberty and the pursuit of happiness set forth in the constitution. Even though slavery was divinely wrong, it was legally right, so therefore legally correct to persecute a person because of their race.

From these and other incidents, along with forward thinking men and women began the steps toward the abolition of slavery. Many states, such as Vermont, Pennsylvania, and Massachusetts, had already banned slavery as early as the late 1700's. States in the west or Midwest like Illinois, Kansas, Michigan, Wisconsin and others were established as "free" states. However, this presented a problem that mimics police practices that exist to this day.

As time progressed, there would be an influx of "freed" black men. Whether they were freed by their masters, worked to purchase their freedom, escaped to free territory, born in a free state, or just born free (there were many who were free and thriving even during the height of slavery; don't ask me how), they lived and prospered during these eras. However, they were still subjected to the whimsical targeting of their white peers, whether law enforcement or not.

Freed black men were supposed to carry "freedom papers" at all times. These documents served as proof of the carrier's liberty. If the papers were not present or deemed to be unofficial, the black man could be jailed or even worse, sold back in slavery.

Many times, even if the papers were legitimate, black men still could be overruled by the white officer or citizen. Freedom papers were often stolen, burned, or confiscated. As portrayed in the fact-based movie, "Twelve Years a Slave," a free black man was duped out of his papers while drunk and sold into slavery by his white companion. This incident shows that even freed black men's rights weren't even respected by the main society.

The conditions of black men in this period mirrors a practice that was prevalent a couple of decades ago and in some respects still is today. The "stop and frisk" procedures made popular by New York and L.A. policeman, are eerily similar to the requests by white slave patrols for freedmen's papers.

In the 1980's, 1990's and even today, black men were disproportionately stopped by officers, searched and detained. Their basis for these actions, were that the subjects looked suspicious. Being that most of the suspects were black, it seemed that the only criteria for suspicion, was skin color. Similarly, the only requirement for free black men in 1800 to be accosted by white men or police was skin color.

No other situation reflected the American judicial and legal position towards black men clearer than the Dred Scott decision. Scott was a slave in 1830 who was taken by his master to Illinois, which was a free state. He also lived in Wisconsin and Missouri, also anti-slavery states.

In 1846, after his owner's death, he sued the master's wife for his freedom. After a victory in lower court for Scott, the decision was appealed to the Supreme Court by his new master. In 1857 the Supreme Court ruled against Scott. The decision stated that slaves or descendants from slaves are not entitled to the rights of a citizen and therefore had no standing in court. In layman's terms; "a black man has no rights that a white man was bound to respect by law."

This judgement reflected the mindset of most white men of the day. As time progressed, perspectives began to change regarding the inhumane institution of slavery. It may have been the threat of violence toward slave owners. It may have been the guilty conscience of masters spurred on by the riveting speeches of abolitionists. More probable, just like anything else in this country, economics were the reason most white men of that day, wanted to put an end to slavery.

In the south, where slavery thrived, agriculture was king. They made their income off tobacco, cotton, sugar, and other farming products. Due to slave labor, their output was minimal. They only had to purchase a slave once, and they would have a lifetime employee.

The more industrial centered northern states were not so fortunate. Instead of paying $300 dollars for a lifetime worker, they had to pay each man $300 a year to maximize production, which minimized profits. The barons of the north grew envious of their southern counterparts and suggested they end slave labor to level the playing field. The southerners refused and the battle lines were drawn.

In April of 1861, the beginning of a grueling four-year war commenced. Two groups of white men basically fought and died over their right to control or not to control other human beings. Over 600, 000 men, mostly white, died in the Civil War, which is touted as the bloodiest war ever to be fought on American soil.

In the middle of the affray, President Lincoln issued the infamous Emancipation Proclamation in January 1963. Contrary to popular belief, this document didn't free many slaves at all. It only declared that slaves living in Free states and those not under Union control were to be considered free from then on out.

The ironic part is that both the North and the South enlisted black men to participate in this conflict. The southerners commanded their slaves to fight in defense of their continued captivity. The North enticed freed black men and runaway slaves to join the efforts in liberating their fellow kinsman. This was a further display of the white man's propensity to dominate the Negro, even during times of war.

With both sides at odds, the status quo was maintained by the state. The militaries made sure that no freed man or slave was unaccounted for. The slave patrols were still in full effect. Freedmen's papers were still demanded at the drop of a dime. Ultimately, black men still had no rights that white men were bound to respect.

Finally, in April of 1865, the brutal war ended. The North emerged victorious, while the South were broken and defeated. Southern states that seceded from the Union were admitted back upon their abolishment of slavery. So, in the year of 1865, slavery officially ended.

However, with years of deep, ingrained hatred and control of another human being, conditions and attitudes of dominance would persist. Southern whites detested seeing their former slaves walking around with freedoms they once denied. Northern whites were fearful of the influx of freed black men who were migrating amongst them to take their jobs and livelihood.

Even the great President Abraham Lincoln had his reservations. He once said, "If I had been able to save the Union, without freeing the slaves then I would have (Baysler)." This statement proves that the highest officer in the land still did not hold blacks in the same regards as himself. As we shall see in the next chapter, measures were soon put in place by lawmakers, and enforced by police that continued to keep black men oppressed for the next hundred years.

Chapter 2

The Criminalization of Color

As slavery ended, there was a sense of loss of control from the white society. Blacks were free to move around unrestricted and enjoy liberties like everyone else. The white men were used to dominance. Fearful of the black man's physical and mental ability to excel, they begin to institute law, discrimination, terror and outright violence to ensure that they remained in a position of power.

The first of these measures was the Ku Klux Klan in 1865. This organization was a group of citizens who donned white sheets and hoods to hide their faces. Dressed in disguise, they descended upon black communities, houses and persons, normally in the middle of the night to exact terror, violence and fear.

The Klan entered houses and dragged men and women out into the darkness, many times never to be seen again by their families. They raped, burned down properties, pillaged land and goods, threatened, lynched, and hung the defenseless black citizens. Their trademark, a cross burning in the yard, usually spelled disaster for the occupants of the property.

Ironically, the Klan was pegged as a good Christian organization. When the members took off their regalia, they returned to their everyday life. The church pastor, the city doctor, the mayor, sheriff, the police chief, the county commissioner, the banker and the grocery store owner were all card-carrying members of the Klan. The victims had no escape from their tormenters. The men in disguise would never convict themselves of any wrongdoing after the night was done.

A second component of subjugation for freed blacks by the American system was the ratification of the 13th amendment to the Constitution. This happened only eight months after the Civil War. The new amendment stated that slavery was illegal except that a person was duly convicted of a crime. Then it was perfectly legal to use that person for the purpose of free or slave labor.

This provision was significant because of what happened next. The white power structure knew that since they made laws and enforced them, they could ensure that blacks would be convicted of crimes, which would return them to forced labor. So, states begin to pass laws that made it nearly impossible for blacks to exist without breaking the law.

This was accomplished by the introduction of the Black Codes. The Black Codes were a set of statutes aimed at blacks that made life hard or easy to get arrested. There were several different types of laws, but I will only expound upon a few.

The most common was that blacks were forced to sign a yearly labor contract to work for whites for small wages. If they refused, they were fined, arrested, and eventually forced into unpaid labor. These contracts were a way for the former slave owners to ensure a cheap workforce.

Some states required Negroes to have written evidence of employment at the beginning of each year. If they couldn't provide it, then they were arrested. Other states enacted laws that said blacks couldn't work in any capacity other than a farmer or servant. This further reduced skilled artisans to either servants if they complied, or criminals if they refused.

Other states had more limitations on black life. Codes included not being able to work, marry, own property, testify in court, make contracts, and even be certain places at certain times. These laws essentially made it a crime to be black and in pursuit of life, liberty and happiness; the rights given under the Constitution.

The exception clause in the 13th amendment became relevant. If blacks refused to work for whites and worked for themselves, they were arrested. If they had no work or no home, they were arrested for vagrancy. If they attempted to buy property, marry, live where prohibited, looked a white man in the eye, spoke to a white woman, or committed any of thousands of other minor offenses, they were arrested.

Not only were they wrongly convicted of the smallest of crimes. The guilty blacks were given an unlawful amount of prison time. A man who stole a chicken from a farm may receive a twenty-year sentence. A homeless man who drowned his troubles in liquor may be sentenced to thirty years hard labor. A black man accused of lying to his employer may be remanded to life on a chain gang.

These laws were enforced by all white federal, state, and local police officials. Even all white militias, who were usually made up of the same people, had the ability to arrest, try, and convict people of color at will. Angry mobs of white men were known to storm courthouses and jails, usurp the police's authority, and drag prisoners out into the streets to administer their own justice, which was normally death. Back then, just as many feel today, blacks had no one to turn to when treated unjustly.

Despite the odds stacked against them, many blacks still managed to thrive during this era. They resiliently carved out locations away from white society, built businesses, homes, stores and bustling communities. However, many times, whites who couldn't fathom their former subjects living better than them, found a reason to come and destroy everything that the former slaves had built.

The most famous of these incidents happened in Tulsa, Oklahoma in 1921. Black residents of the Greenwood district succeeded in establishing a self-contained area free and independent of white control. The area of black owned churches, schools, banks, hospitals, stores and other entities was so prosperous, that it was dubbed, "The Black Wall Street."

Soon, the inevitable happened. A common cause of white instigation against blacks occurred. A black man was accused of attacking a white woman.

Some say the black shoeshine boy tripped while entering the elevator and fell into the white woman. Then she screamed assault. Others say the black man and white woman were consensually involved. When another white man saw them riding the elevator together, which was forbidden, she screamed rape. Whatever the case may be, the simple accusation of a white woman towards a black man was enough to incite the masses of white men against the all black community.

White mobs were organized. White vigilantes were provided with weapons and deputized by the city government. When they went to the jail to lynch the accused, armed black men prevented the kidnapping. During the confrontation a shot was fired, and chaos ensued.

Later that night, white mobs entered the black neighborhood burning and looting property. Even aircraft was used to drop bombs on churches, schools, stores and homes. After two days, more than 10,000 blacks were left homeless, 800 were hospitalized, about 300 left dead and today's equivalent to 32 million dollars of property damaged or destroyed.

This was considered the largest "race riot" in United States history, but certainly not the last. Two years later, in the all black town of Rosewood, Florida a similar incident occurred. As I mentioned earlier, the common claim of a black man assaulting a white woman was the cause.

After hearing the claim, dozens of armed whites, do doubt sanctioned by the governing authorities, stormed the all black town shooting and killing citizens. When one brave man fired back, killing two of the vigilantes, hundreds more white people joined the attack.

The terror lasted for about four days with an unknown, or unreported number of blacks killed. The towns businesses, churches, homes, and property were all burned to the ground or destroyed. Just like in the Tulsa case, and many police shootings today, a grand jury found no evidence of wrongdoing by the whites, and no one was charged with the murder of blacks or the destruction of their property.

Another occurrence in Washington D.C. in 1919 followed the same narrative. A white woman, Bessie Gleason, claimed that she was attacked by two black men who tried to take her umbrella. She reported the lie to her husband, who was a sergeant in the military, and pandemonium followed.

The man rounded up his fellow soldiers, who took to the streets in full uniform and terrorized black citizens. For five days, police stood down while the white men committed violence against blacks. Even the Washington Post recruited more whites to join the ruckus. Law enforcement only stepped in when the blacks began to defend themselves and they took the side of the lawless whites.

The continuous propagation of the big black boogeyman by whites is essential to the state sponsored slaughtering of black men. Whether it was the Scottsboro Boys case of 1931, the white woman's claim of Emmitt Till's flirting, the Central Park jogger's case in the 80's that wrongfully convicted five black teenagers, Susan Smith who drowned her kids and blamed it on a black man, or Hillary Clinton's labeling of black men as "Super Predators." Even the "Karen" agitators of today are reminiscent of things past. False narratives, stereotypes, and allegations have always been used to incite law enforcement against African men.

Sometimes, there was no provocation needed. As in the case of Wilmington, North Carolina in 1898, whites in power were jealous of the government in the all black town and wanted to dismantle it. Once more, the black man's plight to life, liberty, and happiness, was prohibited by the state government.

The incident was instigated and planned by Charles B. Aycock, a democrat who would become governor of North Carolina three years later. He organized a band of barbarians, descended on the town, burned down businesses and newspapers, murdered at least 60 blacks and overthrew the locally elected government and replaced them with racists.

This attack was part of a larger pact by influential men to preserve white supremacist control throughout the state. I cringe when I think of the yearly field trips to Charles B. Aycock's birthplace in elementary school. Thousands of black children unknowingly paid homage to a self-proclaimed racist in the name of education.

The power structure was always able to justify their raids through media. Mainstream newspapers always portrayed blacks as the instigators and whites as the restorers of order. This concept gave the racists whites a sense of bravado and allowed them to be boastful about their exploits. White sentiment for black suffering was at an extreme low.

A major influence in desensitizing white acts of violence towards blacks was a 1915 movie. "Birth of a Nation" was based on a novel called "The Clansman," written by a self-proclaimed white supremacist named Thomas Dixon Jr. Dixon was labeled a professional racist and held positions as a politician, lawyer, playwright, lecturer, novelist, and filmmaker. He even served a stint as pastor at First Baptist Church in my hometown of Goldsboro, North Carolina.

Dixon's book, and D. W. Griffith's subsequent movie, portrayed black men as violent, unintelligent and sexually aggressive to white women. In response, the Ku Klux Klan would ride through the land in heroic fashion rescuing their women from the savage blacks by killing them. After the viewing of this movie, it was said that enrollment in the Ku Klux clan nearly doubled.

The fact that governors, pastors, military, police, newspapers, and average white citizens had no reservations about committing violence towards blacks individually and collectively, speaks to the fabric of this nation's attitude. The State sanctioned violence against blacks today and non-prosecution of such acts is nothing new. White supremacist racism is as American to the people of this country as apple pie.

The terrorization continued for nearly 100 years after the Civil War when former African slaves were so-called "freed." Eventually, blacks and conscientious whites reached a point where they were tired of the hypocrisy of America. This ushered in a period of civil unrest, where those against the inhumane treatment of blacks upset the natural order. The next chapter will explore this era known as Jim Crow and Civil Rights and how the white power structure managed to stop progress using governmental measures.

Chapter 3

Police Suppression Civil Rights

After nearly a century of oppression, discrimination and degradation, blacks and white sympathizers started to petition and strategize for equal treatment. In the 1950's the federal government and presidents enacted orders that abolished the black codes, Jim Crow laws, and segregation that had kept blacks subjugated. They were finally getting their respect as human beings and citizens of this great country…or so they thought.

Even though federal laws were passed guaranteeing blacks their inalienable rights, they still faced opposition on the state and local levels. Two main issues were the integration of schools and the ability to vote. They would be the source of conflict between law abiding citizens and police and even military forces for the next two decades.

In 1954, a decision was made by the Supreme Court to integrate public schools. The case of Brown versus The Board of Education made it illegal for segregation to exist in the school system. Despite the fact, local and state governments continued to operate in defiance of laws. Anyone that attempted to enforce the order was met with violent and sometimes deadly force.

An infamous event shed light on the still heinous nature of some whites. In Little Rock, Arkansas, in 1957, a group of nine students from an all-black school were selected to attend the all-white school of Central High. The group, infamously dubbed "The Little Rock Nine," approached the school grounds on September 3, of that year.

Instead of open arms, welcoming teachers, and excited school staff, the young black scholars were met with the Arkansas National Guard. The military men were flanked by an angry, threatening and screaming mob. Ushered away on that day, the attempt to enter the school was made again three weeks later. The students did gain entry, but the victory was short-lived. They again had to be rescued to safety after violence erupted and their lives were threatened.

A similar incident gained national attention to the south of Arkansas just six years later. In New Orleans, 1963, a six-year old girl named Ruby Bridges was slated to be the first African American girl in an all-white school. Once more, she was met with angry mobs protected by police. She made several attempts amid threats of death to her and her family. Finally, she was able to enter the school, much to the chagrin of the local white power structure.

While federal laws were constantly being changed to afford blacks equality, state and local entities continued to deny them. One example of this was the infamous George Wallace, governor of Alabama in 1963. In his inaugural speech he declared he would not integrate, and proclaimed "segregation now, segregation forever (Blackpast)." He even employed the state national guard to block two black students from entering the University of Alabama, after a supreme court gave them access.

These are just a few incidents of many regarding schools where states and municipalities ran by racist white men used the police force to deny the rights granted to blacks. Many used law enforcement officials to outright prevent the quality of life for blacks. Other times, police were complicit in ignoring the actions of those who mistreated citizens of African descent.

Despite constant opposition, determined blacks kept fighting against the state sponsored oppression. In February of 1960, a group of students in Greensboro, NC defied the unfair ordinances of the time. For five months they entered the Woolworth Department store and sat at the counter reserved for whites only.

Their courage set off a string of events nationwide. Across the country, blacks started to push the envelope. They began to enter once forbidden businesses, demand fair treatment and service, and assert their rights as American citizens. Although they paid for it at times with incarceration, violence, and even their lives, often at the hands of police, their resilience began to get results and garnered the attention of the nation and the world at large.

Another obstacle that blacks faced was the ability to vote. Since the political process was run by the majority racist white power structure, they were constantly turned away from the polls. Literacy tests, lack of property ownership, residency proof, poll taxes and many other tactics were used to prevent the casting of black ballots. Many times, potential voters were met with outright violence by police or military to stop them from voting.

In the face of this opposition, many advocates and leaders arose. The most renown was a young Baptist minister from Atlanta, GA. Martin Luther King was a charismatic, fiery speaker that used his eloquent verbiage to captivate audiences and arouse them to action. Other famous people like Adam Clayton Powell, Paul Robeson, James Baldwin, Malcolm X, Jim Brown, Muhammad Ali, Kareem Abdul-Jabbar, Bayard Rustin, Dick Gregory and many others used their voices to bring attention to the plight of blacks in America.

King was able to obtain support from many different groups. The NAACP, the SCLC, SNCC, CORE and other organizations all joined forces to fight systematic racism. With this coalition, King and others comprised mass demonstrations and marches to disrupt order, and make the power structure uncomfortable.

One such event was the march from Selma to Montgomery, Alabama. In March of 1965, King and a mass group of demonstrators set out on the 50-mile trek to the state capital. The efforts would soon be thwarted by Governor Wallace and his racist, segregationist ideology.

At one point during the journey, King's group was met by a legion of Alabama state troopers who advised them to turn around. When they refused, the law enforcement officials attacked the defenseless, non-violent men and women with nightsticks, tear gas, dogs and even whips. Many victims were beaten severely, bloodied, and jailed for their stance. The matter was caught on tape and eventually broadcast to the world.

Though this event may be the most notorious, it is certainly not isolated. Many such violent eruptions were recorded in other places. There are videos that show police forces in full uniform beating with batons, punching, releasing police dogs, and spraying black men, women and children with fire hoses. Those images of public police brutality endorsed by the government are eerily similar to the barrage of videos displaying the murder of unarmed black men by police today.

Nevertheless, through the agitation, marches, protests, and speeches, their voices were eventually heard. The violence by the police in response to peaceful protest proved to be too much for the American public to stomach. In August of 1965, President Lyndon Baines Johnson passed the Voting Rights Act. This move outlawed the many discriminatory practices used against blacks to negate their participation in the election process.

Despite laws to the contrary, blacks continued to face persecution by individuals and civil entities. Due to the continuous struggle, various groups, leaders and organizations emerged to advocate for justice. In addition to the NAACP and SCLC, other non-traditional, non-conforming ideals emerged.

One such organization was the Nation of Islam or the Black Muslims, as they were known to whites. The religious organization was led by Elijah Muhammad and spearheaded by an eloquent, dynamic, blunt minister named Malcolm X. The Nation preached a self-sufficient concept of separation from the white man's government and economic system. They established their own businesses and even trained their members for protection. These trained men were known as The Fruit of Islam and served as the Nation's military arm.

Another group that served to fight for equality and justice was the Deacons for Defense and Justice. In 1964, this organization was started by Ernest "Chill Will" Thomas and Frederick Douglass Kirkpatrick. Based in New Orleans, the members formed to protect each other from the violence inflicted by the Ku Klux Klan. Out on the west coast about two years later, a like-minded group of young black men started a similar organization. In October of 1966, in Oakland, CA. Huey P. Newton, Bobby Seale and Elbert Howard established the Black Panther Party for Self Defense. The Panthers believed in the ideologies of socialism, Black Nationalism and self-defense. Contrary to popular belief, they were college educated scholars, who knew the law and were not afraid to let the power structure know it.

With all the unrest, organization and political pressure gauged to end racism, the government began to fear these young black leaders and speakers. In order to combat the movement, the top law enforcement official in the land, J. Edgar Hoover, began his plan to destroy these groups. As the head of the Federal Bureau of Investigation, he developed an agenda called COINTELPRO that would lead to the death of some of the greatest black thinkers ever.

The counter-intelligence program (COINTELPRO for short) was designed to target, sow dissension and discord, confuse, and outright assassinate this new young breed of brash outspoken black men. This was done through illegal wiretaps, unwarranted surveillance, paid and confidential informants, framing them for uncommitted crimes and on some occasions, murder. Once more, America's highest law enforcement agency was used to unfairly and unjustly target its black constituency.

One of the first major assassinations was that of Medgar Evers in Jackson, Mississippi in 1963. Evers was a World War II veteran who worked for the NAACP. He was very active in the fight for civil rights and assisted in getting witnesses in the Emmett Till murder trial. For his efforts, Evers was murdered in his driveway by a white supremacist named Byron De La Beckwith as he exited his car.

While the shooter seemed to be acting alone, one cannot rule out government or police complicity. History has proven that the government has used patsies to accomplish their dastardly deeds. Nevertheless, De La Beckwith was arrested for the crime. After two trials that ended in a hung jury, he was released and wasn't retried until thirty years later. In 1994, he was convicted at the ripe old age of 72. The failure to prosecute the murderers of black men in this country is nothing new.

Popular opinion holds that the F.B.I. and the government had a hand in the assassination of Malcolm X in February of 1965. Before his death, he had split with the Nation of Islam amid tensions between him and the leader Elijah Muhammad. Documents have surfaced of government wiretaps and informants in both camps. Even letters were sent to sow discord, jealousy and contention between the once close companions. If the bureau didn't directly pay the hitmen that killed Malcolm, they were responsible for creating the atmosphere that led to his demise.

On April 4, 1968 the shot heard around the world was fired. Martin Luther King Jr. was killed on the balcony of the Lorraine Motel. A 40-year old white male, James Earl Ray, was tried and subsequently convicted of the crime. He was sentenced to 99 years in prison and died nearly 40 years later.

However, all throughout his life, Ray maintained his innocence, claiming he was just a patsy. Considering all the wiretaps, surveillance and informants the F.B.I. had placed around King, his story seemed plausible. Finally, in 1999, only a year after Ray's death, the government admitted responsibility in the murder of King and paid his descendants a huge settlement. This is another example of the state being responsible for the death of an innocent black man.

There are many other lesser known assassinations and murders of black men in this time period. Whether they were activists or ordinary citizens, lynchings, beatings, rapes, framings and murder, were a constant peril for blacks all over the nation. These acts were perpetrated by law officials, judges, prosecutors, governors, mayors, police officers and other upstanding white citizens. Sometimes they were done under the disguise of the Ku Klux Klan. Other times it was done in the performance of their everyday civic and professional duties.

As we see from this chapter, no matter how many laws and orders were passed to guarantee blacks equal rights, the government still failed to protect them. From the agents assigned to famous leaders, to the National Guard that prevented integration, to the state and city policeman that brutalized, terrorized, and murdered, the long arm of the law was always against blacks. Even the legislative bodies were just as guilty, refusing to arrest, prosecute, and convict those guilty of crimes.

The actions of the U.S. political and criminal justice systems of the 1950's and 1960's are similar to that of today. Why has so much changed, yet so much has remained the same? The next few chapters will show how the overt targeting of black men has morphed into the covert operations that exist to this day.

Chapter 4

Destruction of Black Power

The Civil Rights era caused a fear in the white power structure. They saw blacks began to galvanize support for their cause through protest, boycotts, speeches, riots, resistance and structure. The young charismatic leaders influenced the masses of blacks to stand up against the oppressive racists. This is the reason they had to be silenced.

The murder of Malcolm X and Martin Luther King Jr. was not enough. J. Edgar Hoover, the head of the F.B.I., was considered the most powerful man in America at the time. With his unlimited government resources and unchecked power, his agenda was in his own words, "to prevent the rise a black messiah who could unify and electrify the militant Black Nationalist movement. (Hoover)."

Although he "neutralized' the more popular targets, many others sprang up in their wake. The fuse had been lit and blacks started to take pride in their blackness. Gone were the days of kneeling while some white racists cracked you over the head until they got tired or began to feel guilty. This new breed of leaders taught self-defense and armed resistance.

When the civil rights movement failed to provide lasting change in black communities, a group of student activist came together. In 1966 the Black Panther Party for Self Defense gained traction. They implemented a 12-point program to uplift their community on several fronts. Due to their success in Oakland, several chapters sprang up around the United States.

The Panthers were truly for the people. They organized a free breakfast program to feed underprivileged children daily. They fed the elderly, sponsored schools, provided legal aid, clothing, transportation, healthcare services, and many more resources to their community. They even stood against the distribution of drugs and police abuses of power. For residents, BPP (Black Panther Party) headquarters were a one stop shop for any and all services.

Their focus was police brutality. In California, like most places at the time, police were extremely aggressive towards blacks. Many departments recruited southern whites and ex-military to serve. These officers had disparaging views of blacks and showed it in their treatment.

To combat this, the BPP formed police surveillance patrols. Armed with legally registered guns, the Panthers followed police and observed them within safe distances in the performance of their duties. Whenever an officer abused his powers or broke the law, they would step in, law book in hand, and make the officers adhere to the statutes. This interference caused ill will and conflict between the panthers and police.

The F.B.I. took notice. The Panthers were named as one of the greatest threats to national security. A smear campaign began, painting the organization as communist, Marxist and socialist, all terms deemed to be in opposition to the American way of life. Add on the militant label and the possession of guns, and the BPP became the white power structure's public enemy number one.

The Panthers became the subject of constant harassment and surveillance from police. Their demonstrations were interrupted, programs targeted and everywhere they went, the police were present. In April 4, 1968, just two days after Martin Luther King was killed, the first member of the BPP was assassinated by the police.

While riots raged all over the country, Panther leader Eldridge Cleaver, 17-year old Bobby Hutton and two other members were stopped by police. A gunfight ensued and two officers and Cleaver was wounded. The leader and the "Lil Bobby" fled to an abandon building where they had a standoff with police for 90 minutes.

With Cleaver severely suffering, the teenage Hutton eventually surrendered. He stripped down to his underwear and walked out with his hands raised.

Despite the obvious act of submission, Bobby was shot by police twelve times and died on site. The police later claimed that Hutton emerged wearing a trench coat and tried to run away while reaching for a weapon. No officer was charged in the cold-blooded murder.

This case is reminiscent of the Mike Brown murder nearly 50 years later. The teenager was reported to have had his hands raised high, when he was shot by police. The officer would later claim that Brown attempted to grab his gun and he feared for his life. To further demonize Brown, a video surfaced of him snatching cigars from a store owner and pushing the smaller man out of his way.

Due to the constant vilification of the victim, just like in Hutton's case, the officer in Brown's case was acquitted. The media's portrayal of Brown and Hutton as criminals and dangers to society, made it easy for the public and the judicial system to classify their death as justified, even though they posed no deadly threat. Malcolm X put it plainly in a speech 50 years ago.

"The controlled white press inflames the white public against the Negro, and the police are able to use this to paint the Negro community as a criminal element. The police use the press to make the public think that 99% of the Negroes are criminal. And once the white community is convinced of this, then this paves the way for police to move into the negro community, using gestapo tactics, stopping any black man on the streets...as long as he is black, the white community feels that the police is justified in trampling on that man's civil rights and his human rights (Enpazconpaz)."

Malcolm's words echo in the wake of recent public murders of black men in America. He didn't live in this day in age, but his assessment still holds true. There is no difference in these media and police tactics from then until now. The criminalization of the black man allows the infringement of his rights just as much in 2020 as in the 1960's.

Another black panther, Fred Hampton of the Chicago chapter was a victim of this familiar targeting. In 1967, he was marked as a radical threat by J. Edgar Hoover and the F.B.I for his leadership and his organizational skills. He formed the Rainbow Coalition, a group of people from all races. He taught political action courses. He was also orchestrating a merger between the BPP and a large street gang called the Black P Stone Rangers, led by Jesse Jackson's half-brother Jeff Fort.

Because of his influence, he had to be stopped. Hoover began sending false letters to sow discord amongst fellow panthers and the other groups Hampton was involved with. He created racist literature and distributed in the BPP's name to alienate white supporters. They even enlisted informants to infiltrate Hampton's chapter. One would become Hampton's bodyguard and set up the event that would take Fred's life.

On December 4, 1969 at 4:00 a.m. a raid was executed on Hampton's house. It was led by a tactical unit from the Cook County's State's Attorney's Office, the Chicago Police Department, and the F.B.I. The police entered shooting Mark Clark who was on a couch in the front room. He was the security detail and was killed instantly.

Then they proceeded to the bedroom where Fred Hampton lay asleep with his girlfriend, who was nine months pregnant. The officers forcefully removed her from the room and then fired a shot at Hampton wounding him in the shoulder. They then dragged him out of the bed and fired two shots at point blank range into his head. His body was then laid on the floor in the pool of blood.

Several other party members were shot during the raid. The officers claimed that they were fired upon while knocking on the door. However, studies, investigations and eyewitness testimony contradict this account. As usual, no officers were charged. The murder of Hampton was deemed justified.

Not only were members of the BPP killed, they were also framed and jailed for long periods of time for crimes they didn't commit. In 1973, Panther Geronimo Pratt was convicted for the murder of two white people and received life imprisonment. F.B.I. COINTELPRO documents indicate that he was set up by the bureau.

Arrested two years after the murder, Pratt was targeted because of his political beliefs. The F.B.I. orchestrated the trial, interfered with the jury and coerced witnesses. They even withheld wiretap information that proved that Pratt was in Oakland the day of the murders, and not in Santa Monica where they occurred. Even a bureau agent confessed 25 years later that Pratt was framed. Twenty-seven years after the trial, the conviction was overturned, and Pratt was released.

Throughout the 1970's many more members of the BPP across the country were harassed, arrested, and unfairly prosecuted by the U.S. judicial system. Assata Shakur was arrested between 1973-1977 for murder, attempted murder, armed robbery, bank robbery and kidnapping for six separate incidents. She was acquitted on all charges. Then in 1977, she was convicted for murder of a police officer, where she was a passenger in a car that was involved in a shootout with police. In 1979, she escaped and still lives in Cuba to this day.

In 1970, a student, Angela Davis was arrested for assisting a prison escape. George Jackson and other defendants were on trial, when his brother took over the courtroom and tried to free them. A judge and two officers were killed along with others. Angela Davis was arrested for providing the guns. After a year and a trial, she was found not guilty. George Jackson eventually was killed in jail, reportedly by the hands of guards.

Then, there were the constant legal battles of Huey P. Newton, Eldridge Cleaver and Bobby Seale who were the leaders of the Panthers. They were charged with everything from inciting riots, contempt of court, conspiracy against the government, rape, attempted murder, murder, kidnapping, and assault. Most of these charges were dropped or overturned, but this served as the government's method of destroying their reputations and their messages.

When framing members of the BPP wasn't enough, the F.B.I. disrupted the effectiveness of the organization by creating dissension, envy and jealousy within the Panthers and between other groups. Letters of misinformation were distributed to leaders with slander, lies, and malice enclosed. This led to rifts between the likes of Huey Newton, Eldridge Cleaver, Bobby Seale, Stokely Carmichael and many others, weakening their structure.

The F.B.I. also used this tactic to pit black organizations against each other. The Panthers, Organization US, The Black P Stone Rangers and other groups were victims of this sabotage. Panther member Ralph "Bunchy" Carter was killed by members of Organization US because he reportedly made derogatory statements about their leader. Conflicts like this destroyed the unity and weakened the overall strength of the black power movement.

Even on the east coast, the police were intolerant of black liberation organizations. In 1972, John Africa founded the MOVE organization in Philadelphia, PA. This group resembled the BPP. They advocated for human rights, and lived life secluded on their own compound. They were self-sufficient and separate from government control.

In 1978, the police demanded entrance to the compound and a shootout ensued. Eyewitnesses say police fired the first shot, but reports maintain that members of MOVE fired first. After a standoff, the members surrendered, were jailed and tried for murder. Nine people were convicted and sentenced to 100 years in prison.

After numerous attempts to shut down the movement, MOVE eventually changed locations. In 1981, they were labeled a terrorist organization and constantly surveilled and harassed. In 1985, warrants were issued for members of the group on charges from parole violations, illegal possession of firearms, to making terroristic threats.

On May 13, 1985 police descended on the residence and ordered the members to exit. They turned off water, electricity and vacated nearby occupants. When members refused to exit, a bomb was dropped on the facility, killing eleven people including five children. The survivors were charged with crimes, but no law enforcement agency was punished.

It was acts like these described in this chapter that informed the black public that the government would not allow them to exercise their rights to stand up against oppression. It was made clear that they were to stay in their place, and allow the white power structure, via police, to keep their foot on their necks (i.e. George Floyd).

With all the pressure of the late 60's, 70's and early 80's the black power movement eventually died out. Many of the leaders were dead, in jail, exiled, or disenfranchised by political oppression. All this dismantling was spearheaded by the police after the criminalization of black organizations. Just like in the days of slavery, Jim Crow, and segregation, to be black was to be an enemy of the state. With blackness demonized, the state could now further criminalize and subjugate the black man with a new weapon.....drugs.

Chapter 5

The Crack Era

Though Hoover's COINTELPRO destroyed the major revolutionaries of the day, some lesser known groups survived the carnage. These groups did their best to maintain the liberation spirit. But their efforts were no match for the powerful government and law enforcement agencies.

One black organization that endured the 1970's intact was the Crips. Started in the mid-seventies by Raymond Washington and Stanley "Tookie" Williams, their initial goal was to uplift the community. Even the name Crip was an acronym for Community Revolution in Progress. Like the Panthers before them, they would quickly be targeted for criminalization and destruction by sinister methods.

Another "gang" formed in the 1970's were the Bloods. Founded by Sylvester Scott and Vincent Owens, their name stood for Brotherly Love Overcomes Oppression and Destruction. With a similar objective, the Bloods were very organized and respected as an influential entity in the black diaspora.

While the Bloods and Crips were on the West Coast, various other black groups sprung up. In Chicago, the Black P Stone Rangers were founded by Jeff Fort. In the same town, the Black Gangster Disciples were started by Larry Hoover and David Barksdale. With the young products of the black power movement coming of age and gaining traction, a government intervention was eminent if history was to be any indication.

Enter the dragon. Crack cocaine was the highly potent, addictive form of powdered cocaine that could be smoked. It was made from heating the raw powder into liquid, then adding substances like baking soda, ether and other additives to make it hard. Resembling little stones or pebbles, the finish product was given the nickname of "rocks" and could be smoked in glass pipes, soda cans, pill bottles, weed and even cigarettes.

It is well-known today that the government, via the C.I.A., played a major role in distributing not only crack, but also guns, to lower income black neighborhoods. This revelation was uncovered by reporter Gary Webb of the San Jose Mercury newspaper in 1996. The articles, "Dark Alliance," detailed the connection between the C.I.A., Nicaraguan drug smugglers, the Iran contras, and L.A. street gangs, in crack distribution and profits. Eight years later, the whistle-blower Webb was found dead in his apartment with two gunshots to the head.

Webb's work before his demise was very telling. It focused on one, Ricky "Freeway" Ross. Ross was a young black dealer who was introduced to cocaine by his teacher of all people. At the age of nineteen, he started selling the drug for his teacher, but soon became one of the major dealers in Los Angeles. Although illiterate at the time, he had a knack for business and eventually got connected with his teacher's supplier.

Oscar Danilo Blandon Reyes was a Nicaraguan refugee who fled to the United States in 1979 after the overthrow of the government. Upon his arrival, he started to raise funds for the Nicaraguan Democratic Force, which was a contra group backed by the U.S. government. His method of fundraising was distributing cocaine and guns to urban cities.

It was in this capacity that he met Ricky Ross, via his teacher. In 1981 Ricky or "Freeway" began to traffic large amounts of cocaine for Reyes. With an unlimited supply, Freeway expanded his operation into several states and cities across the country. At the height of his operation, Ross boasted an income of three million a day.

Although the profits were rolling in, Ross was unknowingly sleeping with the enemy. Reyes, his supplier, was a C.I.A. informant who was on their payroll. He used his profits from drug and gun trafficking in black communities at the government's behest, to fund the U.S. backed Contra rebels in the Nicaraguan civil war.

However, both Freeway and Reyes were disposable. Years after the government accomplished their goals they charged Reyes with conspiracy to distribute cocaine. He was sentenced to four years. When he agreed to set other dealers up, his sentence was reduced to two years.

Upon his release, he entrapped Ross to buy 600 kilos of cocaine. During the transaction, Ross was arrested and faced life in prison. He received twenty years and was released in 2009. This is an example of the way it would go for black men during the next few decades. The major players like Reyes, oftentimes government operatives, would ride off into the sunset, while pawns like Freeway would spend the better part of his life encaged.

Reyes and Ross are just one of many cases of foreign drug traffickers allowed to distribute drugs to inner cities with the assistance, permission, or impunity of the U.S. government. Throughout the 1980's there was an influx of immigrants from South or Central America. Columbian, Peruvian, Mexican, Dominican, Panamanian, and many other cartels flooded urban communities with their gross national products...cocaine. The government watched in silence as they reaped the benefits in a bevy of nefarious methods.

The movie "Scarface," featuring Al Pacino was a depiction of the 1980's cocaine explosion into the U.S. The 1983 Oliver Stone film depicted a Cuban refugee, Tony Montana, who rose to power in Miami by distributing massive amounts of cocaine. With his South American connections, they wreaked violence and calamity while paying local, state, and federal judges and law enforcement officials to let them operate. This movie would become a fixture in the urban community as young, impoverished, impressionable black males aspired to become rich and powerful like Scarface through drugs and violence.

How did this portrayal and the actual existence of crack and guns in the urban community affect its members? Young men, who were already disenfranchised, disillusioned and disengaged, jumped at the opportunity to take part in the American Dream they had been so long denied. The gangs that once for protected the neighborhoods began to distribute drugs and fight for territories in a lust for money and power.

Many will say that the drug users, dealers, killers, and gangbangers that emerged in the Reagan era were savages, predators, and menaces to society. While I don't condone the acts or behavior and realize the detriment that crack had on those involved, one must not overlook the government players, policies, and paradigms that caused such conditions and circumstances to come about. When a people have been demeaned, degraded, and demonized for so long, they soon began to accept the labels and act accordingly.

At the onset, people didn't know the addictive powers of crack cocaine. It was just another party drug, like weed, pills, LSD, powder and the like. However, a few years after its introduction into the mainstream, the destructive effects would take the urban community by storm.

Users soon became full-fledged "fiends," a person who would do anything for crack. Sunday school teachers turned into prostitutes seemingly overnight. Businessmen traded their upper-middle class condo, for a couch in a "crack house." Little Johnny, who loved playing basketball transformed into a teenage drug dealer after both of his parents got addicted and abandoned him. The local mechanic lost his shop after he began pawning auto parts to support his habit. Normal people's worlds came crashing down at first usage.

Crack addiction was not just restrained to the black community. White judges, lawyers, congressman, mayors, stockbrokers, real estate agents, ball players, priests, soccer moms, detectives, and people from all walks of life used. From the White House to Wall Street, no one was immune. Despite this, the news media and in turn law enforcement only focused on the damage that the black communities suffered.

So instead of showing white businessmen who embezzled hundreds of thousands of dollars to support their addictions, the news only highlighted gang shootings and drug infested areas in black communities. Instead of reporting the breaking and entering, larceny and fraud of white users, crack babies, armed robbery suspects, and prostitutes of African descent constantly graced the news. Suddenly, black people became the face of the crack "epidemic."

In response to public fear and outrage, a term resurfaced that was made popular in the 1970's. The government declared a "War on Drugs" at that time in response to heroin and opioid usage. Now the term was used as a stance to the growing exposure of crack cocaine to the entire country. However, there were two previous campaigns used by the government to popularize drugs to those who had no knowledge of them.

In the early eighties, Nancy Reagan coined a term while speaking to a group of elementary students that would serve as almost an advertising campaign for drug usage. "Just Say No," urged children to resist things that they had not yet come in contact with. This phrase was all over the schools, in commercials, on billboards, in newspapers, and on the news. I remember as a child constantly hearing about this mysterious monster called drugs.

To piggy-back off that message, another program, D.A.R.E., was introduced to school age children across America. In 1983 the LAPD started the Drug Abuse Resistance Education. This consisted of police officers entering classrooms with various drugs, informing children what they were and how they affected the body. Once again, children had a firsthand view of substances they would probably otherwise never see.

While the intentions were noble in theory, this may have had an adverse effect on the participants. With children being young and impressionable, there was a natural curiosity. I recall myself being enamored by the mystique surrounding drugs when I attended these sessions. As many parents can attest, as soon as you tell a child not to do something, they rebelliously disobey. Considering the amount of my peers that were using or selling drugs as early as the sixth grade in the early 90's, the program created a desire to use drugs whether than resist.

As a result of these campaigns and others, people all over the country were being informed of this threat to society. This propaganda led to the reemergence of the declaration of "The War on Drugs." Even though polls at that time showed that

Americans didn't think drugs were the biggest problem, Reagan still declared that illegal substances were public enemy number one.

A decade earlier, Nixon made the same declaration behind unscrupulous motives. One of his top leaders stated, "We knew we couldn't make it illegal to be black, but by getting the public to associate blacks with heroin and then criminalizing them heavily, we could disrupt those communities. We could arrest their leaders, raid their homes, break up their meetings, and vilify them night after night on the evening news. Did we know that we were lying about the drugs? Of course we did (Hanson)."

This blatant plot by the government against blacks, echoes Malcolm X's statement in the earlier chapter. This is what was done to the civil rights participants in the 60's, the black power groups in the 70's and the recipients of the drugs and guns deliberately dumped in their neighborhoods in the 1980's. Once they have made blacks the face of the problem, then they could go into the communities and do what they want all in the name of law and order.

And invade the communities they did. Regular police forces were given military gear. S.W.A.T. teams were formed and given army tanks with battering rams. Warrants and illegal search and seizures were executed on potential drug suspects

[69]

with the precision and aggression of a Beirut task force. Police became occupiers of neighborhoods and the residents were reduced to prisoners of war...The War on Drugs.

Nothing depicts this policing policy in America more than the city of Los Angeles in the 80's and 90's. Police misconduct, brutality, aggression and abuse ran rampant in communities of color. Police chief Darryl Gates deliberately recruited officers from southern states like Mississippi, Alabama and Georgia who held racist views and had little contact with blacks. These officers in turn entered the urban communities with the Gestapo tactics that Malcolm mentioned.

Incidents of excessive force grew more prominent, culminating in the infamous Rodney King beating in 1992. In the face of scrutiny, Gates continued to defend his officers. A decade earlier, he was defiant in the face of outrage over multiple blacks dying at the hands of officers using chokeholds, i.e. Eric Gardner. His response, "blacks are more likely to die from chokeholds because their arteries do not open as fast as they do in 'normal people (Altman).'"

Gates' statement is reminiscent of the government, police, and white power structure's view concerning black people from slavery to now. To consider a person not normal is to open the door for justified mistreatment of that individual. This injustice that was magnified in the big city of L.A. was equally prevalent across the country. Although the methods were a little more covert, major cities on the east coast were also suffering from police occupation of their neighborhoods.

An infamous New York case brought attention to police misconduct in 1986. Larry Davis, a 20-year old black male from the Bronx, was the victim of an assassination attempt by the NYPD. When they raided his home to kill him, he defended himself. In the affray, six officers were wounded, and Davis escaped. After a two-and a half week manhunt, Davis surrendered in the same housing project the raid occurred.

A few years earlier, Davis, who was a popular neighborhood deejay with many friends, was approached by police. However, it was not because he'd done anything wrong. These officers solicited the high school kid to sell drugs for them because of his popularity. Seeing an opportunity to make money, he took the chance.

The operation went well until Davis grew tired of the game. When he told them of his intention to quit, they harassed, intimidated and threatened both he and his family. When the officers grew more aggressive, Davis threatened to turn the officers in to their superiors. With their lives and freedom on the line, the corrupt police took matters into their own hands.

To silence Davis, they planned to frame him for the murder of a local drug dealer they had killed. On November 19, 1986, the corrupt officers descended upon Davis with attempt to serve the fraudulent warrant. Larry, fearing for his life, opened fire and escaped.

During the trial, Larry's lawyer, William Kunstler, presented evidence of police corruption and complicity in drug-dealing. He contended that Larry's abandoning of them in the illegalities were the reason for the raid and murder charges. Larry Davis was subsequently acquitted on the charges of attempted murder of six police officers. He was then found not guilty of two murders the police tried to frame him for. However, while serving a five-year sentence for gun possession, he was convicted of a third murder and sentenced to twenty-five years. Davis was killed in prison in 2008 from multiple stab wounds.

The fallout from the Davis situation was far reaching. Many came forth with testimony that highlighted the black experience with police and corroborated Davis' story. A few years after his conviction, a group of cops from New York were convicted of conspiracy to sell drugs, robbery, civil rights violation, extortion, perjury and other felonies. The "dirty thirty," as they were called, remain an example of the corruption and brutality of policing in American Urban neighborhoods.

Another case that highlights the criminalization of blacks was the Central Park Five. In April of 1989, a white woman jogger, Trisha Meili, was raped and assaulted while running in a park. After spending days in a coma, she awakened, not remembering what happened. Despite having no evidence, the police arrested five black youths under the age of sixteen.

All five were convicted and sentenced to years in jail. After finishing their penance, the true attacker, Matias Reyes, a serial rapist confessed to the crime. His DNA matched and the five were exonerated after completing their sentence. They eventually sued the state and received millions for their trouble. However, their lives and legacies would forever be scarred.

Although the last incident has nothing to do with drugs, it alludes to the theme of this chapter that all blacks are considered criminal or immediately classified as a suspect whenever a crime is committed. Just like in years before, the courts and government use the black man as the face of crime, whether he is guilty or not.

The two high profile cases of Ross in L.A. and Davis in New York are just two of many examples of government and police involvement with the imprisonment of blacks. However, just as with sports and entertainment, as those cities go, so goes the country. The treatment and handling of black life by police and the judicial system, set precedent for small towns all over the U.S. to implement procedures and practices that mirrored the two major metropolises.

The stage was set. Stereotypes were solidified. Prejudices were prevalent. Biases were believed. The constant use of the phrase, "black on black crime," subconsciously associated blacks and crime as synonymous. Fear of the drug using, drug dealing, gang banging, violent young black man was foremost in the mind of America. He was public enemy number one and the police were commissioned do any and everything to stop him from destroying the country.

The media propaganda associating drugs with black men was a success. Soon, "stop and frisk" became commonplace. Illegal searches were conducted without penalty. Racial profiling became a normalcy for every black man who lived in America. The result was the "New Jim Crow" or the new slavery...the mass incarceration of black men in the United States Prison systems.

Chapter 6

The Clinton Crime Bill

Following the carnage of the 1980's crack era, the early nineties brought a new sense of consciousness. Black leaders and entertainers started to speak out against the destructive effects of drugs, guns, and gangs in the black community. Moreover, information began to surface on how the government was instrumental in causing the influx of drugs and guns into urban areas. Like the 70's people started to resist.

The major source of resistance was in the music. Artists like Queen Latifah, Brand Nubian, KRS ONE, Poor Righteous Teachers, Public Enemy, Arrested Development, and countless others, began to spread the message of self-love, heritage and pride to the black youth. Songs like "Unity," "Fight the Power," "Self-Destruction," "We All in the Same Gang," and others promoted oneness, peace and strength to the hearers. Just the names of some of the groups exuded a sense of consciousness.

I remember this era vividly. I was twelve or thirteen just entering Jr. High school. Me and my peers sported Malcolm X shirts and African medallions around our necks. We grew afros with the black power fist hair picks. We embraced our blackness with Kente cloths, scarves and head wraps. Black pride was gaining ground.

Then, seemingly overnight, things changed. Suddenly, there was a new phenomenon called gangster rap. This new breed of emcees was brash, aggressive and cocky. Instead of condemning the issues plaguing the community, they glorified and romanticized gun violence, drug use, distribution, gangbanging, materialism, self-genocide and degrading women. This genre of "Gangster Rap" took the country by storm and captivated young people of all colors, creeds, and class.

By the time I got to high school in 1992, black power and pride had evaporated. Rappers like N.W.A. (Niggas with Attitudes), Dr. Dre, Snoop Dog, Tupac, Notorious B.I.G., Mobb Deep, Jay-Z, The Geto Boys, Ice-T, and many other encouraged us to sell drugs, shoot guns, live lavishly, have sex with multiple women, smoke weed, and die young. The lyrics and beats, along with invigorating videos influenced us to mimic the rappers' portrayal of life.

Soon, I and my peers, who once wanted to go to college and be ball players, engineers, accountants and the like, either wanted to be rappers or live the lifestyle the rappers promoted. We were smoking weed, drinking, and peddling weed in school or crack in the streets. We wore the gold and brands of the rappers, carried the type of guns they touted and tried to sleep with every girl we could. Music had us mesmerized.

For anyone who would negate the influence of music over culture, I would offer this quote. Scottish politician Andrew Fletcher stated, "give me control of a nation's music and I care not who makes the laws (Ward)." These words emphasize the power of music and how it supersedes the logical thought process, especially in youth. A deeper look into who controlled the music industry at that time will explain the change in content of rap music from the 80's to the 90's.

There are only six major corporations that provide 90% of the media in the U.S. Of these six, Universal, Sony, and Warner are very involved in the music and film industries. These labels are household names and can be found in the credits of movies, records, and a myriad of other productions. However, proceeds from endeavors were not enough as executives of these companies embarked on a diabolical scheme to increase revenue while destroying lives.

In 1991, at the height of the resurgence of black consciousness in rap music, the heads of the major music labels held a secret meeting with their employees. Also attending this meeting were members of the Corrections Corporation of America

(CCA), a private entity that purchased state prisons. After acquisition, the facilities were then privatized for profit and able to be traded on the public market.

The record label employees and higher ups were informed that their employers for had just made a major investment in the CCA. Their job was to now ensure a return on the investment. To accomplish this task, they had to use the very influential rap genre as a tool.

A requirement for CCA to purchase a prison was that it had to maintain a minimum 90% occupancy rate. The newly formed partnership of prison companies and record labels would rely on the glorification of violence, drugs, and crime through rap to induce behaviors conducive to their plan. The more criminality they projected, the more money they made.

They also had to rely on police, lawyers, prosecutors and judges to target, pursue, over-prosecute, and over-sentence those black males that fell victim to the plot. This three-pronged attack worked to perfection.

The A & R's (artist and repertoire) of the record companies went to work with only dollar signs in their eyes. The conscious, knowledge purveying, good time having, fun-loving and happy artists were quickly shelved. The companies scouted new artist or developed existing ones into the drug dealing, gun-toting, weed-smoking, high rolling personas that we saw back then, and today.

Along with the music, these media conglomerates also used the big screen to promote crime. The early 90's featured an influx of movies that depicted the black male as the perpetrator of all things wrong in America. Movies like "South Central," Menace to Society," "Juice," "New Jack City," and "Boyz in the Hood," displayed characters who were violent, drug-dealing robbers and killers. So not only did the movies influence black life, they also presented the image of the young black male as a negative part of society. This was social engineering at its best.

Enter Bill Clinton, the smooth talking, saxophone playing, ladies' man, from Arkansas. When elected in 1992, he said all the right things to have black people eating off his fingertips. Little did we know, two years later, he would enact legislation that would obliterate the already fragile black community.

Amidst all the media coverage and hype over drugs and crime, Clinton did what politicians before and after him had done. He took a stance of being tough on crime. His response to the problem was the now infamous "Clinton Crime Bill." Its effect was so damaging, it is a source of debate in an election nearly thirty years later. Present

Democratic presidential candidate Joe Biden still faces backlash due to his part in drafting the bill.

This maligned bill had many detrimental consequences. An aspect of the bill that speaks to the plot to fill up prisons was an 8.7 billion-dollar allotment. This large amount was provided to states for the construction of prison sites. However, the only way a state could receive this money was to implement "truth in sentencing laws."

These laws required an inmate to serve eighty-five percent of a sentence for violent crimes. Essentially, states received money to build more prisons if they guaranteed inmates would serve longer sentences. Additionally, this also helped the CCA's mandate that the privatized prisons remain 90% full.

This 356-page bill also provided for 100,000 new police officers. These excess forces were deployed to urban areas as a part of the Community Oriented Policing Service (COPS). Police sub-stations were placed in public housing and low-income areas, making it easier for law enforcement to target, profile and eventually arrest people of color.

Increased police presence brings more arrests. With more arrests, comes more prosecution. More prosecution equates to more convictions. A higher conviction percentage amounts to more sentences, leading to more people in prisons.

Indirectly, this increased police force was and is responsible for the mass incarceration issue that we see today.

Another damning aspect of the Clinton crime bill was the "three strikes law." This mandate required a defendant who was previously charged with a felony, be sentenced to twice the amount of time that the offense warranted. A third infraction after two felonies induced a harsh sentence of 25 years to life. This law included non-violent drug offenses, which guaranteed prisons would have a steady flow of labor for decades to come.

While these inmates were serving long sentences, a proponent of the bill ensured that they would have a higher chance of returning to prison upon their release. This legislation eliminated the offender's ability to receive higher education in the form of degrees or trade skills. Having not improved their capabilities, the inmate is more likely to return to crime on the outside. This may explain the recidivism rate of 85% at one point. Since the goal of the private prison sector is to keep the prisons at maximum capacity, the results were welcomed.

Many more provisions of the 1994 crime bill devastated urban communities. The ban on assault weapons included semi-automatic rifles, pistols, and shotguns that were already largely available in black neighborhoods and in possession of many soon to be offenders. Being caught with these firearms resulted in several years in prison.

The Federal Death Penalty act, another part of the legislation, provided 60 new offenses eligible for capital punishment. In addition, fifty more federal crimes were added, including making membership of a gang a federal offense. Domestic violence laws were heightened, and drug testing became mandatory for all federal inmates released on probation. There are many more damning elements of Violent Crime Control and Law Enforcement Act of 1994 that still yields harrowing effects twenty-five years later.

The reason this legislation was so instrumental because it was the culmination of years of pre-conditioning to arrive at a desired end. As Nixon's quote in the last chapter indicates, it was essential for the government to equate the black population with crime and drugs. This view was not only held by him, but by leaders in power during the Clinton era.

In 1996, two years after the crime bill went into effect, first lady Hillary Clinton allowed her true feelings about young black men to slip. The then president's wife used the term "super predator," when referring to black male teens (Lee). She went on to describe them as having no conscience and no empathy. With political figures speaking as such, the general public would see no issue with locking up thousands of blacks at an alarming rate.

With statements like Hillary's and decades of negative propaganda, the nineties paved way for the crime bill to dissipate the black community by incarcerating or placing millions of black under the control or supervision of the United States judicial system.

Today, there are more black men in prison and on probation or parole that the amount enslaved in 1865 at the end of slavery. More telling, there are more men in entrenched in the criminal justice system than there are in all the colleges or universities in the country. Many people discount this as just the way it is or justify it by blaming the offenders for their behavior or for the environment their forced to exist in. However, one must consider all the factors in this chapter and the previous ones before passing judgement.

Being that I came of age in the 1990's I witnessed the effects of this crime bill first-hand. Being sixteen at the time the bill was launched, I, as most people, had no idea of the repercussions of the laws, agendas and campaigns that were being instituted. It is only in retrospective reflection and research that I realize the importance of the era that I matured.

The war on drugs was nothing more than a concentrated effort to make money and expand law enforcement capability by the criminalization of a culture. Even today, states, cities, counties, municipalities, jails, and prisons, all receive government funding based on the number of people they incarcerate.

Across the country, officials benefit off the continuation of crime. Judges gain reelection based on how many people they send to jail. Prosecutors move up the ladder by how many convictions they secure. Police chiefs and sheriffs retain their position by how many arrests their officers make. Mayors, Senators, Governors, and Attorney Generals all boost their statuses off the public's opinion of their stance on crime. However, ending crime is the last thing on their agenda.

In order to keep this farce going, there must be a steady queue of criminals to impart into this system. Contrary to the popular belief, criminals are not naturally born. Most of the individuals that eventually commit crimes are socially engineered and conditioned to fall into this behavior pattern. Next, we will examine how fun-loving, innocent children are transformed to hardened criminals, seemingly overnight.

Chapter 7

School to Prison Pipeline

Throughout my childhood and early teen years, I consistently heard how the deck was stacked against boys who looked like me. Teachers taught me that black men had less of a chance to make the age of 21 than others. Statistics said that one in three black males will end up in prison. Then, I thought something was wrong with me. Now, I realize that it was the way things were designed to be.

Despite the odds, I was fortunate. I was considered academically gifted and placed in classes with mostly white students. The teachers treated our classes with favor and leniency because we were prized students. Even so, as I got older, I noticed that the teachers treated me and my peers different than my white counterparts.

Disciplinary measures seemed to be harsher towards the children in "average" classes. Even the few blacks in the gifted rooms were judge more tightly than others. A white student, who challenged teachers were tolerated. When I did it, I was labeled disruptive and corrected differently. As I noticed the difference, my attitude and behavior changed accordingly.

Just like today's urban schools, most of the teachers were middle class white women. With the majority of children being from low income families, there was a natural disconnect. Not being able to relate or communicate effectively with unruly or challenging children or teens, the teachers' only recourse were to send them to the principal's office.

As with the judicial system, once a child got labeled as troubled in the school system, the reputation followed them. From elementary, to Jr. High to High School, their disciplinary records were available to teachers, counselors and administrators. With the preconceived negative perception, these students were given a much shorter leash, with less room for error.

After numerous write-ups and visits to the principal's office, troubled students faced a bevy of consequences. One of these was after school detention. This is where the pupil was detained after school ended for the day. They'd be confined to a classroom and given extra assignments or duties. Just the mere mention of the word "detention" denotes a certain message, as I have spoken at a few juvenile detention centers in my time. In retrospect, this form of punishment may have conditioned and prepared some students for those facilities.

A second form of discipline very prevalent in elementary and junior high school was in school suspension (ISS). Students sentenced to this method of punishment were resigned to a separate class for the entire day. Time limits were three, five, ten or even permanent for some students. The teacher in this class was very strict and enforced stern rules.

I experienced this punishment in the six and seventh grades. We were made to sit at a desk with barriers on three sides. We couldn't see, talk to, or interact with other students. We were only allowed to leave our seats at lunch time, where we were the only children in the cafeteria. We were completely isolated from everything and everyone. Having been to prison and jail in my adulthood, this experience is eerily reminiscent to those stints of confinement.

The third and probably most damaging method of discipline was suspension or expulsion. This is when the student is not allowed to attend school at all. These periods were three, five, ten days or indefinite. The absences were not excused and counted towards the maximum days allowed to be missed in order to be held back from passing the grade.

Suspensions were devastating in many ways. First, they put the student behind in their work. Many of the children with behavior problems also had trouble comprehending. Coupled with a lack of structure and assistance with assignments at home, inevitably led to disinterest and hopelessness in learning.

Additionally, the child that acts out in school normally comes from a home without a lot of guidance. On suspension, the child may be left to his own devices. The age-old adage that an idle mind is the devil's workshop becomes true. The unmonitored child is left to things like truancy, vagrancy and petty crime that will start a long perilous descent into the criminal justice system.

The third factor that makes suspending at-risk students dangerous is that the record of suspensions will follow them throughout schooling. Students who miss too many days because of suspensions are either left back or eventually expelled. The child who flunks faces ridicule from peers and self-loathing that can lead to conflicts with others and acts of misbehavior. The child who is expelled is left to roam the streets, susceptible to more trouble. Or, they can attempt to be enrolled in another school, in which their negative track record precedes them. He then goes to a new setting with a target already placed on his back.

In my day, the kids who were deemed intolerable for regular school had another option. In the early 90's, alternative schools were set up by the administration. These institutions were reserved for students expelled or referred by teachers who could not or would not deal with them. These facilities had very strict regulations and isolated the students from interaction with their "regular" peers.

The students attending alternative school carried a stigma. They were considered outcasts, losers, and castaways. They couldn't attend regular school functions like dances, proms, play sports, and some were even banned from attending games or stepping foot on campus. By the time they reached this juncture, these much-maligned children had become disillusioned with the entire process. Dropping out or bucking the rules of the school was inevitable.

When a student or teen had exhausted all resources at the alternative school, they were eventually sent to "training school." These were facilities away from their home, where they went to live and as I thought then, to be educated. Unbeknownst to me, these places were nothing more than juvenile detention centers, or more bluntly, child prisons.

The residents of these centers could have landed there in numerous ways. They may have committed petty crime offenses, had trouble with their parents who sent them away, or in the way I described above. Since going to school as a minor was required by law, minors who were forbidden to attend school were placed in violation of the law. This lead to judicial intervention, blemishes on their record, and the subsequent placement in the training school.

It was as early as 5th or 6th grade when I started to see the "troublemaking" students disappear. They would be out of sight and out of mind, until their name emerged in conversation. Then it was realized they had been sent to Dobbs. Dobbs Youth Development center was located in Kinston, NC, the next county over.

From elementary to early high school, students would leave and return. Upon their reentrance to school, they displayed a certain bravado; a chip on their shoulder. They seemed manlier, more rigid. Something had changed that wasn't there before they left. They had more of a disrespect or disdain for authority. Having spoken at these centers and spending time in Polk Youth Center in Raleigh at the age of 21, I now understand why.

Confinement is unnatural and inhumane. However, if one has been subjected to it for long periods, he adapts. They began to normalize the structure and almost crave it. This is what some call being institutionalized. They accept the fact that someone has complete control over when they eat, sleep, play, shower, and interact with others.

Another thing that changed the youth was the violence. In close quarters, with energetic, frustrated, testosterone filled pubescents, conflicts

[90]

arise. Fights are commonplace. If one doesn't defend themselves, he ultimately becomes prey for others. When one does, he gains a reputation and others ambitiously test it. Fighting becomes the mark of manhood in this kill or be killed environment.

So, when the juvenile delinquent returns to school, he has all these bad habits formed in the facility; laziness, dependency, violence and aggression. This makes it harder to function in a regular organized setting; like a prisoner returning from a 10-year sentence. They bragged about all the fun they had at Dobbs, who was still there, and how they wouldn't mind or don't care about going back.

Sooner or later, they would do so. I remember guys who returned for a period of only two weeks, only to do something to be sent back. They had become institutionalized, unable to function in the regular constraints of society. Sadly, all the peers who went to training school as children also went to prison as adults. Many had long sentences, multiple stints, and some are even still going and returning to and from prison today.

Another method of criminalizing students began my sophomore year in school. The administration instituted a policy that resulted in criminal charges against a student who got in a fight. Yes, for a normal teenage act the police were called, warrants were sworn, and court cases were set.

Once more, this led to regular, everyday students having a criminal record before leaving high school. It was if the powers wanted to introduce children to the court system at an early age. Even I was charged with affray in the eleventh grade, after a 20 second scuffle with a fellow student. Luckily, we both agreed to drop the charges. This was my first experience with the judicial system, but not my last.

Another drawback to the American education system is the curriculum. Malcolm X was once quoted as saying "only a fool will let his enemies educate his children (X)." Most studies agree the most important aspect of teaching is acknowledging the background of the student. In teaching a child, you must teach them about themselves first, and then the culture of others. All these statements relate to the inefficiency of the education system towards black males.

Malcolm's statement is not directed at the individual instructors. Even though eighty percent of all public-school teachers are white, they have little to no bearing on what they teach. The statement refers to the educational institutions that serve a governmental system that has continuously shown to be an enemy of the black race. As school psychologist Dr. Umar Johnson, exerts, "you can't expect people who have oppressed you to give you knowledge that will allow you to rise from under their oppression (Cannon)."

It has been well-documented over the years how most tests are culturally biased and designed in a way harder for blacks to pass. The SAT's, ACT's, SOL's, CAT's and other intelligence and IQ tests are comprised by a mostly white constituency, with bias, prejudice, or disregard for people of color. This results in low scores for blacks, which in turn justifies and promotes the stereotypes of blacks being inferior mentally.

There is a drawback to the percentage of white teachers compared to black students. Many of them come from upper middle-class white suburbs and have no regular contact or relationship with black children outside of the classroom. So, children get labeled unmanageable, uncooperative, or mentally challenged, not because they are so, but because there is a cultural, social, and relational disconnect between teacher and student.

The teacher's methods, communication style, body language and other tactics may be non-compatible or to the child's and vice versa. This leads to frustration, miscommunication and conflicts that may otherwise have been avoided or resolved by someone who can relate to the child on a cultural level. Since that is not so, the child develops the negative reputation that will follow him throughout school into society.

The most damaging act of the educational system in America is not teaching anything of relevance about black, mainly African culture. This has a psychological effect on black students that causes them to act in an inferior way and have an unconscious negative view of themselves. This low opinion manifests itself in a myriad of ways throughout school and adult years.

All I learned, from elementary to High School is about the greatness of white people. George Washington never told a lie. Christopher Columbus discovered America. Abraham Lincoln freed the slaves. Benjamin Franklin discovered electricity. Thomas Edison invented the lightbulb. Isaac Newton discovered electricity and so on and so forth.

We were taught of the greatness of Queen Isabella and King Ferdinand of Spain, King Louis of France, King George of England and King Leopold of Belgium. Explorers like Amerigo Vespucci, Ferdinand Magellan, Marco Polo, Ponce De Leon, John Cabot, Vasco da Gama were glorified for their exploits. The pilgrims, and men like Francis Drake, Walter Raleigh, John Smith and others were praised for their conquests of "The New Land."

Science, English and mathematics were the same as history. We learned of the wonderful works of Albert Einstein, Galileo, Louis Pasteur, Marie

Curie, Charles Darwin and Sigmund Freud. Writers like William Shakespeare, Edgar Allen Poe, Charles Dickens, Mark Twain, John Steinbeck and Emily Dickinson were presented as the greatest people to ever grace a typewriter. Men such as Rene Descartes, Pythagoras, Archimedes and others were said to be the founders of mathematical formulas and theories that changed the world.

When it came to the arts and philosophy, it was more of the same. Leonardo Da Vinci, Michaelangelo, Van Gogh, Picasso, and Rembrandt were propped up as the greatest painters to ever live. Beethoven, Mozart, Bach, and Choppin were taught to have created the finest music known to man. Plato, Socrates, Aristotle, Nietzsche, Voltaire, and Machiavelli, we learned, were the greatest thinkers on earth. According to our textbooks, everything that was anything of value to humankind was originated, conceived or contributed by whites.

Contrarily, when it came to blackness or things African, we were of little to no importance. The only thing that we learned of the African continent in school was negative. The land was full of unintelligent, savage cannibals until the great white colonizers of Europe came and civilized it. This indoctrination caused many blacks in America to be indifferent to Africa and deny any connection to the motherland to this day.

The representation of blacks in America was no better. We were only taught that we were slaves until the great white hope Abraham Lincoln freed us. This created a deeper love for whiteness because it provided a white savior. After freedom all we learned about was the Jim Crow and Civil Rights era, where we were mistreated. After twelve years of this teaching, unconsciously, the idea of blacks as second class humans was implanted in the minds of many.

However, the information about blacks and Africa could not be further from the truth. The books failed to mention that the captives who arrived in the bottom of boats were not slaves at all. They were architects, engineers, farmers, mathematicians, astrologers, chiefs, artisans, masons, philosophers, scientist, doctors, herbalists, ironsmiths, stonecutters, and kingly knowledgeable men. They were only made slaves upon arrival. Their skills and knowledge were exploited to build this country from the ground up.

The curriculum also failed to expound upon the great exploits of African Kingdoms. The Mali, Songhai, Cush, Egyptian, Aksum, Punt and Mutapa empires were some of the strongest and most influential civilizations to ever exist. They didn't teach us about the great African leaders like Mansa Musa, the richest man to ever live, or Amenhotep, Ezana Axum, Sundiata Keita, Osei Kofi Tutu, King

Menelik II, Haile Selassie, Steve Biko or many other greats. They didn't mention how the Africans ruled the world for 15,000 years and traveled to Europe to help the uncivilized Caucasians survive the dark ages. There was no study of how Timbuktu had the first library and university where the whole world came to study. No mention of how the scholars of today still can't decipher how the pyramids were built. The curriculum didn't mention how they Africans were the first to develop writing and math systems, the first to measure time and develop calendars, or the first to study the solar system. They didn't teach how Africans were navigating back and forth to and from the Americas as early as 700 A.D., or how the Olmec statues in South America prove that Africans came to America centuries before Europeans.

There is much more knowledge I can interject here but to make the point. These one-sided narratives, histories, and curriculums are very detrimental to the non-white student. After years of being denied self-knowledge, an introspective person begins to either search for answers elsewhere or become disenchanted with the learning process altogether. I watched this firsthand, as many of the smartest and brightest black male students before and after me, grew despondent with school as years progressed. Even I myself was not immune.

As I stated before, I was always in the advanced class with mostly white students. Around the seventh grade, I was placed in a homeroom with a black teacher named Mrs. Cox. She was very pro black and encouraged me to embrace my blackness, my history and my advanced mind. She pushed me to read more than the books provided at the school's library.

So, I did. By the time I got to high school, I had enough knowledge to know that I wasn't being told the whole story. I developed resentment for the teachers, lessons, and the school in general. I would challenge the teachers on information that was incorrect or only half true. My awakened attitude, led to many disciplinary infractions.

Although I was considered by the principal to be one of, if not the smartest pupil in the school, by the eleventh grade, I was flunking English. It wasn't because of ineptitude. I just refused to complete the assignments. No matter how hard I tried, I couldn't bring myself to read novels like "The Great Gatsby," "The Canterbury Tales," "The Scarlett Letter," and other boring, insignificant books that only featured lily white characters, written by lily white authors.

An example of the sordid nature of English class was the "Adventures of Tom Sawyer and Huckleberry Finn." We were required to read this work by the great author Mark Twain. While interesting, I noticed the only black character in the book was named "Nigger Jim." The audacity of the schools and the teachers to present that book to black students in the mid 1990's is incomprehensible. It was then that I really saw school for it was...an indoctrination process.

To pass English that year, I transferred to a different school. I went back to Goldsboro in my senior year, but by the halfway point was fed up. Like so many before and after me, I dropped out a few months before graduation. However, I went to the local community college, tested out of the curriculum and received a High School Diploma two months before my peers graduated.

This path was travelled by so many young black men in the 1980's and 1990's. A lot of alpha, strong males took offense to being demeaned by a racially prejudiced and biased educational system. It was conditions, not the individual that made it least likely for the black male to graduate high school. Unfortunately, the same conditions exist today, but on a much larger and sinister scale.

The racial makeup of teachers in public schools has not changed. There is still an influx of white female teachers, charged with the instruction of young black children, especially in elementary. Because of technology and the world's paradigm this new breed of young children is more knowledgeable, overexposed and more energetic.

Since there is still an inability for teachers to relate, certain measures have been instituted to place the blame on the children, instead of the educational system. In the 2000's, children who were rambunctious, unruly, disruptive, undisciplined, or displayed too much adolescent energy began to be diagnosed with mental disorders. Diseases like Attention Deficit Disorder (ADD), Attention Deficit/Hyperactivity Disorder (ADHD), Oppositional Defiant Disorder (ODD), Conduct Disorder (CD) and a host of other non-quantifiable sicknesses emerged.

Symptoms of these diseases include not listening when spoken to, easily distracted, difficulty remaining seated, doesn't finish tasks, temper tantrums, blaming others, not playing quietly and several other childhood traits. Everyone reading this should recognize these as normal, everyday characteristics of any five, six, seven or eight-year-old child and even some adults. By this definition it seems that children were and are being marginalized, labeled, and diagnosed for just being children.

These "symptoms" do not represent a mental disease or a disorder. This failure to control one's actions as a child is mostly attributed to a lack of discipline. I would have loved to disobey teachers, talk back, refuse to sit down, and do all these other actions. The only difference was I knew that I had a father at home, who would not be pleased and would bring swift retribution for my transgressions. Most of these children that displayed misbehavior came from homes where order, structure and discipline were not a priority.

However, maintaining order in the classroom was just the tip of the iceberg for these misdiagnoses. There was an ulterior motive. After being labeled with one or more of the mental disorders, the child was then considered special needs. That categorization was accompanied by the need for an Individualized Education Program also known as an IEP plan. This plan required the child receive special consideration, counselors, and attention to solve the "problem."

Unsuspecting parents began to get their child tested, diagnosed and accepted the results. What they didn't know was that for every special-needs child, the school received extra dividends from the government. Therefore, it became financially beneficial for principals, administrators, teachers and school districts at large to over diagnose these children. The process became less about helping the child, and more about monetary gain. Children were basically sold for profit in exchange for an honest education.

Even worse, the children were often prescribed medicine. Unknowing parents took the advice of trusted school officials and agreed to give their children drugs like Ritalin, Vyvanse, Adderall, Dexedrine, and other powerful drugs. They weren't informed that these medicines were classified as schedule II drugs; the same as heroin, cocaine, opium and methamphetamines. Most of the drugs main ingredients are amphetamines and amphetamine salts.

I've had the misfortune of watching the debilitating effects these drugs have on children. From the ones given Ritalin for being hyper when I was in elementary, to the ones being drugged today, the results are the same. They turn into virtual zombies when the drug takes effect. They are in no shape to think, let alone learn. I've watched some stare off in a vegetative or hypnotic-like state. However, this was good for teachers, who no longer had to worry about the misbehaving student.

As I began to study this issue years ago, I did research on a few of the pills that were prescribed to young black boys I knew. The side effects were life altering and long lasting. High blood pressure, heart disease, testicular issues, loss of appetite, muscle and bone deterioration, vision problems, agitation, anxiety, irritable bowel syndrome, depression, mood swings, insomnia and more, all plague children who have ingested these chemicals for short or long periods of time. The child's physical, mental, emotional, and psychological makeup is being destroyed before he reaches puberty.

More damning than the side effects is the addictive nature of the drugs. Children become almost a slave to the drugs, longing to take them at certain times. I've seen and heard children eagerly ask for their medicine or state that it's time for their dosage. Like any drug, they began to crave the feeling that overtakes them after ingestion.

Two things can result from this. If the child is removed from the drug, they can have serious withdrawal. This can lead to other acts of violence, aggression, depression and even suicide. This reaction can be used to validate more medication, removal from the home, placement in juvenile facilities or group homes, and even legal actions.

Another possible outcome is that the child starts to experiment with harder, illegal drugs as the tolerance for the prescription drugs increases. Of course, this can lead to all sorts of consequences the most probable will be trouble with the law. No matter the outcome, the diagnosing and drugging of young children will surely have a damaging effect on his later life.

Undoubtedly the school systems, just like many other systems in this country, are set up to benefit some and disconcert others. I experienced this with my own daughter in her first few years at an elementary school in Norfolk. The school, St.

Helena, is located in Berkeley, one of the lowest income areas of the city.

I visited the school often for lunch and sat in the class for a while. I noticed things that were very disheartening. The students didn't have textbooks for one. Also, they were not allowed to talk to each other at lunch and were yelled at by an adult monitor if they did. While walking down the hallway, the students were made to place their hands behind their backs, and puff up their cheeks, with a "bubble in their mouth," to ensure they wouldn't talk.

This scene reminded me of the five months I served at Polk Youth center decades earlier. We weren't allowed to talk at lunch or when walking down the hallway. I realized then that these children were being conditioned for prison by the way they were being treated.

When I addressed this situation the principal was rigid. She acted as if nothing was wrong with their policy. As for the textbooks, she informed me that their school barely received enough money from the school board to feed the children. That's when I realized the condition of the school was out of her hands. They were doing the best that they could. I took my issues to the local school board to no avail. I was told by a black administrator that if I wanted to help those children, I should get involved with a local community organization.

After my daughter's third grade year, I transferred her to a school in Virginia Beach, College Park Elementary. This school was in a middle-class neighborhood and had a more diverse population. This school also provided students with Chromebooks, specialized teachers, numerous after school programs and many other amenities.

The disparity between the two institutions illustrates how children from well-to-do families are given what they need to succeed, while the lower income or black schools are left to fend for themselves. This scenario also played out in my hometown of Goldsboro, where most city schools were always struggling for funds and on the verge of being shut down, while the county schools thrived.

The final way the schools have been changed to push children to prison was the removal of the trade programs. As a child, I heard about all of the skilled classes available in high school. Mechanic shop, carpentry, brick masonry, electrician, plumbing and other trades were all classes I looked forward to. By the time I got to high school in 1992, very few if any trade classes were left.

What happened? In the late 70's and early 80's as the drugs moved in, most of the industrial jobs moved out of the inner cities. As more money got allocated to fight crime, there was less funds for education. So the schools, removed the trade programs, while the state built more prisons.

As a result, students who were not scholarly enough for college had no little options. At one time, they could have graduated with a certified trade. Now, they graduated with just a diploma and no viable skills. That's when many turned to the streets to make money, especially with the readily available drugs that flooded their communities.

All the issues addressed in this chapter are not the only reason black males are more likely to go to jail than others. There are many more factors at play that must be dealt with on the other side of the spectrum. Things like lack of discipline, poor family structure, no good role models and other deficiencies contribute to the propensity to lean toward criminal behavior.

However, one cannot discount the psychological effect that twelve years of indoctrination can have on the impressionable mind. From being labeled at an early age, subconsciously belittled through curriculum, over punished for childhood behavior, forced to take drugs and banned from school, the child that has endured this is exasperated at best. He cannot wait to be done with school and enter the real world.

However, since he hasn't been given the proper tools to excel, he enters life unprepared, lost and searching for his position. With little opportunity, not enough scholastic aptitude for college, no job training or employable skills, the average high school graduate has few options.

I'm reminded of a picture of my Jr. High School football team that hangs on my mother's wall. Out of the fifty or so twelve and thirteen year-olds, over half of them had been to prison, jail, or had criminal charges filed against them. These children were no different than any other children in America. The circumstances, conditions, propaganda, laws, and practices somehow gave them a proclivity towards criminality and legal problems. This is not happenstance but occurs by grand design.

Where I'm from, many went into the military. Some took city or state jobs. Others took local factory positions. Some took to the streets to live out the dreams that were portrayed in movies or music, or to live out the predetermined destinies that years of social engineering had caused them to accept.

The next chapters will examine the fate of those who took to the streets and even some who didn't. We'll see how a small-town police force managed to keep the courts and jails filled constantly with young black bodies with the gestapo tactics that Malcolm X mentioned in earlier chapters.

Chapter 8

Target on our Backs

By 1996, the year I graduated high school, I and many of my peers had criminal records. We had already started making our foray into the thug lifestyle. We were drinking and smoking weed on a regular basis, and many were selling weed and crack. Before school began, we would meet the weed sellers in the bathroom, gym, or at the local store to buy weed to smoke just to start our day.

We were entrenched in the allure of street living by the movies, music and news media. Some had older relatives who introduced them to drug dealing at early ages. I remember seeing my first rock of crack at Dillard elementary school. Two classmates were walking down the hall bragging about going to sell drugs on Scaboard St. after school. One of them pulled out a matchbox, slid it open and displayed a small yellowish pebble.

"I'm gonna catch a cab to North End, sell this for twenty dollars and get some more," the novice dealer explained.

I was enthralled by the opportunity of making money that easily. I believe it was that day the hustler in me was born. Four years later as a tenth grader, I was fronted five twenty dollar rocks by a classmate in my Latin class. They were folded up in the outer foil wrappings of Big Red chewing gum. He had received the drugs from a senior classmen who was a big time dealer, as payment for transporting him to buy and sell the illegal substance.

I was supposed to sell the rocks for twenty apiece, grossing a hundred dollars. Then I was to give my classmate fifty, and keep fifty for myself. I tried, but just didn't have the wherewithal to sell the drugs. After about a week, my friend asked for the drugs back. I had failed at my first attempt at hustling.

Disappointed, I resolved to learn everything to know about hustling. I watched all the gangster movies, and listened to as much gangster rap I could. I started hanging at places like the W.A. Foster Center, the "Block," and various projects where the hustlers congregated. I watched, listened, and learned their movements. By the age of eighteen, I was buying my own ounce of crack and selling it in various locations throughout the city.

Let me preface this next section by declaring that drug dealing and any criminal activity is detrimental to society. I will not attempt to justify any behavior of myself or my peers in this era. Nevertheless, just the information set forth in this chapter, along with the facts previously stated in this book, explains the factors that pushed, persuaded, and influenced young black men into that lifestyle then and today.

Nevertheless, former high school students ventured out into the streets in search of the American Dream. Ex All-State athletes traded in gym shorts and college scholarships for crack spots, pagers, nine millimeters and Acura Legends. The hustler became the aspired profession of young men in the 90's all across America; even in the small town of Goldsboro, NC.

In the city, there were several locations one could get their packs off. The "block" was my preferred location. However, many other corners were profitable. John and Pine, Slocumb and Elm, Olivia Lane and Slocumb, Grantham and George, Slocumb and Chestnut, John and Elm and many more were places young hustlers stood and sold drugs daily. The corner stores at these sites, Ward's Package Store, Donnell's, Manhattans, The White Store, Jet's, and others were owned and operated by Arabs, but became the unofficial places of business for dealers all across the city.

Certain neighborhoods and streets were also notorious for criminal activity. The "Jungle," West Haven, Fairview, Lincoln Homes and Seymour were all housing projects were drug flow was prevalent. Virginia, Kornegay, Audubon, Devereaux and Spruce Streets were all avenues that buyers would go to purchase a variety of drugs. It was if the entire city was a cesspool.

Young black street hustlers stood on these street corners or sat in crack houses day and night. A steady clientele of addicts came to get their fix. In the houses, they would sit for hours and buy crack until all of their money was gone. Others would drive through nervously, cop their desired amount, and drive off hurriedly to their destination.

The entire town knew of the drug spots, even if they were not involved in such activity. If the smokers knew where the drugs were being sold, obviously the local police force did as well. In fact, two of the major corners, "the block" and James and Pine, were less than two blocks away from the police precinct. This made for a nice game of cat and mouse between law enforcement and dealers all over the city.

Similar to the stop and frisk policy in New York City, police rolled up on any given set, hopped out and searched anyone at will. To counter this, many spots had lookouts. These were crackheads that stood on corners, and alerted dealers to the presence of oncoming police. Screams of "one time," "man down," "five-O," and "twelves" could be heard for blocks when police were approaching.

When the law pulled up, some would run. Some would stand confidently or defiantly with their drugs hidden in nearby bushes or in empty potato chip bags. Others would not be so fortunate. Surprised, many would be caught with their pants down and searched while they were "dirty." The police would find plastic bags of crack in socks, drawers and small pants pockets and haul the possessor off to jail.

Some would justify this tactic of police by saying that the violators were in drug infested areas. I agree to a point. Just being in an area, does not necessarily mean that one is doing wrong. Legally, these stops violated the fourth amendment protection from illegal search and seizure. Some but not many, would beat their cases in court with a competent lawyer.

Since the majority of these neighborhoods were occupied by black residents, the media association of blacks with crime gave the police department probable cause to execute these searches. They would use any guise for cause; a disturbance in the area, checking for warrants, reports of gunfire, and false intelligence all allowed them to search hustlers or regular citizens in "high crime" areas.

But what makes an area "high crime." It is not the percentage of crimes committed, but the pursuit and the police presence in that area. It is well documented that blacks and whites use drugs, carry guns and commit crimes at the same rate. In fact, the most coveted customers were the rich white smokers who came from the suburbs into the hood and spent the largest amount of money. Today, the most drugged out state in the country is Vermont, the one with the least amount of blacks.

The disparity occurs because the people in affluent neighborhoods and rural areas aren't stopped and targeted as much as those in inner cities. There are not as many checkpoints, raids, stop and frisks, and illegal searches in white neighborhoods. Current presidential candidate and crime bill creator Joe Biden summed up the reason for the difference in targeting in a recent speech; "someone (black) doing crack was fundamentally different than someone (white) sniffing cocaine in a neighborhood as beautiful as this (Dowling)." This mindset of people in power led to crack conviction sentences being a hundred to one in comparison with cocaine in many states.

Essentially, there is a misnomer that blacks commit more crimes than whites that just isn't true. Let's say there's a group of ten white people and ten black people. Out of each group, five people have illegal drugs. However, if only one in ten white people is searched, there's just a 20% chance that you might find drugs. Contrarily, if eight of the black people are searched, you're guaranteed to find at least three people with drugs if not more. This scenario illustrates why there are more black men in the judicial system than whites, and their neighborhoods are considered "high crime" areas. As the title of this chapter asserts, there is a target on our backs.

This bullseye grew much larger with the implementation of the Aggressive Criminal Enforcement Team in 1996. The ACE squad, or the "jump out boys" as they were called on the streets, were a four man unit who patrolled the city in unmarked cars, focusing on "high crime" or predominantly black neighborhoods. The main prey was the low-level drug dealers who lived in these places.

Their tactics were reminiscent of President Bush's "shock and awe" campaign in Iraq. They would cruise the town and surprise their target by turning fast corners, riding up on curbs, hopping out, grabbing, manhandling and searching unsuspecting victims. Those who tried to run were tackled, assaulted and many times beaten severely.

The four man unit soon expanded to multiple cars. Their usual days of attack were on Tuesdays and Thursdays. I still remember the mythological names of the special officers; Tim Bell, Page, and Stapps. The warnings of "the jumps riding today," kept everyone on their p's and q's.

Even though the police and jump out teams would catch individuals with drugs on occasion, these methods still violated the law. The only justification of the illegal, gestapo searches was if drugs were found. If not, the police would just move on to the next point of attack.

This also put others in the community in a precarious position. The fact that law enforcement could perform these illegal searches with impunity under the slightest suspicion, gave them leeway to abuse their authority. The average layperson or black citizen, could be stopped, searched and harassed if they were on the streets in a "high crime" area or not.

I witnessed this recently in my daughter's neighborhood of Berkeley in Norfolk, Virginia. While riding down the street I saw a young teen about fourteen years old walking down the street. The police were driving slowly beside him, pulled over, got out, and stopped the black male. I continued riding, but then decided to turn around and investigate.

By the time I returned, the boy was still walking and the police were gone. I got out and asked the child what the police wanted.

"They wanted to search me for a gun," he replied innocently.

I drove off furious. This incident was a clear case of harassment and violation of that young man's fourth amendment right. Although he lived in a low-income, "high crime," and black neighborhood, he shouldn't have to endure unlawful detainment and searches just because of the color of his skin.

Another way black men were targeted using the "war on drugs" was the indictment method. This is when police used confidential informants, users who were in trouble or actual law enforcement officers to purchase drugs from dealers. After one, or a number of buys, warrants would be issued and everyone who had sold to the undercover would be arrested.

Every six months or a year there would be a roundup of low to mid-level drug dealers. The sweep would happen in the early morning hours to keep the word from spreading through the streets. Charges ranged from sale of cocaine, possession, and possession with intent to sell and distribute. Mediocre bonds were issued and usually the dealers were right back on the streets.

The indictments could also be considered an illegal way of securing charges. Entrapment is the act of tricking someone into committing a crime in order to prosecute them. The police department sending informants into drug areas to buy drugs is nothing short of entrapment and forbidden by law. Nevertheless, this method has been and is still being used to incarcerate many young men throughout the nation.

Another way the legal system incarcerates black males is turning offenders into snitches. Some dealers or criminals will get into legal trouble and elect to help the state convict fellow criminals. The offender would cooperate by providing evidence, information and/or testimony that would implicate other people in the commission of crimes.

In this technique, law enforcement and prosecutors could get two, three, four or five for the price of one. In exchange for assistance, the cooperator would receive a reduced sentence or overall dismissal of charges. This reward system led to more arrests and prosecution, many times on the incredible or falsified witness of a fellow criminal.

Other legislation like the conspiracy laws and the Racketeer Influenced and Corrupt Organizations (RICO) act made it easy for state and federal agencies to attach charges to individuals. A person can be convicted of conspiracy if two or more others say he did something, whether there is any proof or not. A person can be charged with the RICO law if they commit two or more crimes with another person in a certain time period. Then the two can be considered to be running a continual criminal enterprise. These laws, initially installed to bring down mafia families, have been used presently to send mid to high level drug dealers and gang members to prison for life.

As mentioned earlier, this book is in no way an endorsement, justification or an excuse for the criminal activities perpetrated by men of color.

Whether it's drug dealing, gang affiliation, fraud, extortion, robberies, theft or prostitution; all these crimes have plagued the progression of black communities all around the country for years. There is definitely a responsibility and accountability that must be accepted.

However, this work does intend to highlight the absence of equality and equity in the law enforcement and judicial system as it relates to race. Equality is making sure that everyone is treated the same and equity is the surety that everyone is proportionately represented according to their participation in criminality. We all know that these ideas are not applicable in America's judicial system.

An example of the disparity is notated in today's prison populations. Although black men represent about 10% of the nation's people, they are nearly 40% of inmates. In each state in America, the black male prison population percentage doubles their percentage of overall population. Case in point is Pennsylvania. In the Quaker State the 10% black male population boasts a 50% prison populace.

Anyone with two eyes can see the inequality and inequity in these numbers. If everyone uses and sells drugs, commits crimes and break laws at the same rate, then the statistics in the penal and justice systems should reflect that fact, right? However, the targeting of black neighborhoods and men detailed in this chapter and in the entire book make that impossible. The exclusion of other races in the high criminal statistics is a direct result of the failure and refusal to target, arrest and prosecute them in the same manner as blacks.

Now that we've examined why blacks get arrested in higher proportion than others, we can also investigate the courts and sentencing methods. Without this next arm, there would be no mass incarceration. However, we will now learn how the crime bill worked hand in hand with law enforcement and the courts to ensure that the privatized prisons have a steady cache of black inmates to inhabit their facilities.

Chapter 9

Mass Incarceration

After the arrest, the real game begins. A bond is often given and the defendant is freed until his court date. In severe cases an unachievable bond or no bond is given. In this instance the defendant remains in the custody until his day in court.

Depending on the amount of possession, an offender faces various sentencing levels. A defendant may be charged with simple possession, possession with intent to sell and deliver, trafficking in crack/cocaine and conspiracy to commit any one of the previous crimes. The most damaging aspect of these charges is with a conviction, accompanies the lifelong classification of being a felon.

One definition of a felony is a crime, typically involving violence that is more serious than a misdemeanor, usually done with malicious intent and punishable by imprisonment for more than one year or death. Most possessions and sales of drugs are not violent and committed without harm. Yet they are still classified as felonies. The ramifications of this labeling are astronomical and shall be reviewed later in this chapter.

The penalty for simple possession of crack or cocaine can be a slap on the wrist. These charges were usually reserved for addicts who were caught with as little as a dime of crack and as much as a gram. Most charged with this offense would receive a fine, probation, or worst case scenario a few months in jail. Simple possession and possession with intent is differentiated by how the drugs are packaged.

A smoker may have a gram in a single bag all in one piece. However, a dealer may have the same gram, chopped up into five twenty dollar rocks. Therefore, the police will charge him with possession with intent to sell and deliver, rather than simple possession.

The sentence for this offense would be a bit stiffer. A first time offender may get probation. However, most charged with this would get 6-8, 8-10, or 10-12 months. Depending on their previous record, one could get more or less time at the judge's discretion.

An example of a judge over-sentencing was given to me by my mother in the mid-nineties. Ironically she worked for the Federal Bureau of Prisons on Seymour Johnson Air Force Base as a budget analyst. She told me of a teen who got sentence to twenty years for having just seven small rocks of cocaine in Arkansas. No doubt, cases like this happened frequently in places where there was no checks and balances of the courts.

As the amount of drugs increases, so does the sentences. When a person has 28 grams or more of crack/cocaine he is charged with trafficking. It doesn't matter if it was bagged for resale or not. Low level trafficking in my hometown of Goldsboro, North Carolina carries a sentence of 35-42 months. Yes, just for having a golf ball-sized amount of drugs, people are spending three to three and a half years in prison.

Having more than 200 grams, which is about nine ounces can earn the violator up to 10 years of prison time. Over 400 grams, 18 ounces or a half a kilogram can yield a twenty year sentence. A kilogram or 1000 grams of crack or cocaine can result in a life sentence in a state or federal prison.

These drug laws are often used in conjunction with RICO and conspiracy statutes. I know of a man who was set up by an informant. The agent called and asked him how many grams are in an ounce and how much did it cost. Just for answering the question, the victim of entrapment was arrested on conspiracy charges and sentenced to life. Albeit, he did have a lengthy criminal history, twenty years seems mighty excessive for just having a phone conversation.

Federal conspiracy charges are easier to levy and much easier to convict. Federal prosecution can usurp any state case where trafficking is involved. However, they usually reserve themselves for amounts over 200 grams, unless the offender qualifies for the RICO statutes. Federal cases have over a 95% conviction rate and much harsher sentences. The prosecution normally relies on other offenders who have been convicted or who are on trial for their evidence to secure convictions.

In addition to these charges, the judicial system had its own version of three strikes and you're out in North Carolina. When an offender accumulated multiple drug charges over a period of time, he became subject to the habitual felon offense. Three or more felony violations of the same kind warranted this label and carried a sentence of seven to ten years.

The judges, prosecutors and grand juries used this tactic at their discretion also. If there was someone who they wanted but couldn't get on a larger charge, they would implement this charge later to get them off the streets. If there was someone who constantly antagonized police, prosecutors, or judges or who consistently pled out to lower charges for lesser sentences, the habitual felon charge would be added later. Some were even given this charge after three offenses not of the same nature.

After the police have done their job and the charges are stipulated, it is left up to the lawyers and prosecutors to complete the process. Most defendants with mid to high level charges are assigned court appointed attorneys. Even the ones who can afford to hire their own representation, don't get much more bang for their buck.

As mentioned earlier, most of the court cases in America end in plea bargains. The courts rarely want to take the time to select and pay jurors and tie up courtrooms, prosecutors and judges for lengthy trials. They would rather have the cases settled before the docket is even printed. So deals are orchestrated between lawyers and prosecutors during morning coffee, in between golf swings at the club, or over shots of whiskey in the local bar, instead of the halls of justice.

Defendants accept deals for a variety of reasons. One tactic used is the stacking of charges. An offender may be hit with 10 or 20 outlandish charges all at once. They may be frivolous, illegitimate and excessive, but carry very severe penalties. The attorneys will use these charges as leverage for a plea agreement in the following manner.

"If we go to trial, and we're convicted of all charges, you could face 100 years in prison. However, if you plead guilty to the first two charges, the prosecutor will drop the other eighteen and you'll only face four to six years."

To the defendant who doesn't know the law, that sounds like a great deal. However, many times a defendant may beat the charges on a technicality, hung jury, mistrial, or with an efficient attorney. Faced with pressure from their lawyer, family, and their own ignorance, they usually take the deal.

Defense lawyers would oftentimes continue cases for long periods of time, negating a defendant's right to a fair and speedy trial. If an inmate is being held without bail or unable to make bail, each state has a certain length of time to bring their case to trial or it has to be dismissed. The time limit can range from five to seventh months in most cases.

However, the right is nullified when the defense asks for a continuance. This also hinders the defense. With an extremely high caseload, it is difficult for most prosecutors to form an effective case. A continuance in most cases only helps the prosecution get more witnesses, evidence and build a stronger case.

Another way a continuance encourages plea agreements, are the length in which cases may be prolonged; there is no limit. Let's say a defendant's case had been continued for two years, and he's offered a plea of three. Even though he may be innocent or have a viable defense, he may still take the plea. What's a few more months compared to the two years he's served already, or the number of years possible if found guilty.

After the disposition of the cases comes the sentencing and the entrance into the prison system.

Whether called the Department of Corrections or the Department of Public Safety, the warehousing system is not the rehabilitation program that many think. The fact that prisons have been privatized brings a nefarious aspect to this arm of the criminal justice system.

Prisons receive government funding for each inmate in their facility. That income alone keeps the prison running and brings profit. However, the inmates are used as a source of profit within the prison as well. Inmates who work in the kitchen, laundry, landscaping and other prison jobs allows the state and the prison to save money by avoiding the need to hire personnel to complete the jobs.

In return the inmates receive a meager pay of anywhere between 5 and 10 cents an hour. Yes, many prisoners work forty hours a week for less than 5 dollars. This is nothing more than the modern day slavery that Michelle Alexander exposed in her book "The New Jim Crow."

Prisoners also work outside of the prisons. Many states have contracts where inmates pick up trash or cut grass on highways. The prison makes substantial amounts from these deals but still only pay the inmates pennies. This is an example of more slave labor disguised as correction.

Some inmates are privileged enough to qualify for work release. These inmates leave the prison and work regular jobs, usually getting paid less than what they deserve. Then, they have to pay rent and taxes on the money they make. Once again, the prison is making income off the inmate population.

Some prisons take it a step further. Their inmates manufacture products that are sold to private and government entities. Prisoners make military jackets, uniforms, helmets, shoes, electronic equipment, and body armor for the US Army. Some prisons manufacture cheese, fish, produce and juices sold in grocery stores. Everything from jeans, ball caps, park benches, canoes, coffee cups, books and more can be made by inmates making less than twenty cents an hour, while the prisons rake in millions of dollars in profits.

Another method that prisons and jails make money off inmates is providing amenities to use while incarcerated. Detention centers provide canteen, telephone usage, internet service and email services. Some have tablets where inmates can order movies, play music or download games. Other perks include paid video visits, stereos, televisions, and many allow their prisoners to order outside takeout food on a weekly basis. A person with resources can easily spend upwards of a thousand dollars a week while using these outside services.

This privatized system of using inmates as a source of labor and commerce is the underbelly of

America's prison industrial complex. The corporate powers keep this exploitation racket thriving only with the assistance of police, the judicial system and the legislative branch of government. Our correctional facilities have become less about rehabilitation and punishment and more about profitability.

After short or lengthy jail sentences or releases on bond, the ex-offenders would be let back out on the streets. However, with the label of felon and drug dealer, a target still remained on their backs. In a town small as Goldsboro, all of the local law enforcement agencies were familiar with who'd been to jail. So whenever they came across an ex-offender, they would often time search or harass them without reason. After numerous searches, they were bound to find something on them, and it was right back to the system for the defendant.

Another reason the prisons stay so full is the parole and probation system. Offenders are often placed on a supervisory status after being released from incarceration or after convictions The conditions of this mandate requires the person to be free from criminal activity, drugs, remain gainfully employed, perform community service, attend classes, pay fines and supervision fees, and make all appointments. A failure to comply with any one of the terms can result in probation violation and remand the defendant back into custody.

However, many of the requirements oftentimes conflict with each other. It is hard to attend classes, make appointments and perform community service if one is employed. Contrarily, it is hard to stay employed having to be absent from work while completing probationary tasks. In many cases it is hard to find a job having the label of a felon on one's record. This in turn pushes an ex-offender to resort to crime to pay fees and sustain their needs.

The abstinence from drugs also presents a major problem. Many parolees and probationers have had drug addictions for years. They also may have not received the proper treatment in prison or elsewhere. Even with treatment relapses occur and addiction continues. Due to this fact, drug use has been listed as a disease in the DSM-5. So essentially, a violation for drug use is locking someone up for being sick.

Besides the mental health issues of drug use, there also lies the changing of the laws. While some states have legalized marijuana and endorsed it for medical usage, it still remains a violation for probationers. So, there are people still going to jail for using a substance that is legal. The nonviolent nature of drug use has many questioning the imprisonment of users and addicts all over the country.

As mentioned earlier, most offenders must carry the label of felon upon release. This stigma is like a second sentence. One, who has paid their debt to society for past crimes, still faces future restrictions. For this reason, many return to crime in the face of constant opposition when trying to resume a normal life.

The biggest discrimination a felon faces is in the job market. Checking the yes in the felony box automatically disqualifies one from several jobs. Schools, city, state, federal, government, and many corporate jobs forbid felons to be employed in their workplace. This rejection is a source of discouragement and recidivism due to some offenders resorting back to crime.

In addition to income, a felony has a detrimental effect on other walks of life. Many apartments and landlords refuse to rent to felons. Some government programs such as food stamps, healthcare, and other assistance are denied to those with the scarlet letter. Credit companies and banks may even refuse loans to felons. All of these factors create a black cloud over the head of someone who is trying to get over their mistakes.

A felony also makes it illegal for a person to possess a firearm. This second amendment right to protection is nullified, even in the case of nonviolent drug offenses. In my hometown, a person convicted of possession of a firearm by felon would receive a mandatory sentence of 1 ½ to 2 years in prison. These guns are often found in the illegal searches performed by officers who know the offenders and their record.

The felon's life is forever hindered by his status. It reduces him to a second class citizen in many aspects of society. One of the most important aspects of manhood is being able to provide oneself with income and shelter. The denial of this is no different from the slave codes, black laws, and the Jim Crow of years past.

For these and other reasons, the recidivism rates for black men in America are over 50%. For every two black men that are released from prison, one will return. One of the main factors other than the man's poor decision and lack of opportunity after being branded a criminal is the continuous targeting of communities of color. The prison and court systems described here are just another byproduct of America's law enforcement arm's targeting of certain people for years under the guise of law and order.

Now that we've discussed the inequities of police conduct and the judicial system towards blacks, I will now delve into my own personal experiences with the legal and justice system in the next few chapters.

Chapter 10

Unlawfully Detained

It was my senior year in High School. I was a dishwasher at a new restaurant in town, Texas Steakhouse. A few of my classmates were working there as well. I liked the job. Even though I had to deal with dirty dishes, slippery floors, and cleaning rubber mats, I was mostly left alone and unbothered by management. Things were going great until one faithful night.

I normally worked the night shift. I would leave school, maybe hang out with friends and then report to work around 5:30. I would have to stay until the restaurant closed and about an hour or so after for cleanup. That usually had me leaving for home anywhere between 12:00 and 12:30 AM.

The drive home was less than five minutes barring stop lights. Texas Steakhouse was located on Spence Avenue and I and my family lived on Taylor Street. To get home, I could take Spence Avenue until it ended at Elm, make a right on Elm, travel a quarter mile and then make a left on Taylor St. The distance home was about two miles.

On this night, I pulled from the parking lot and headed south on Spence towards Elm Street. As soon as I turned out, I noticed a police cruiser behind me. Instinctively, I switched over to the right lane. The officer did the same. I immediately grew nervous and transferred the controls to autopilot.

I had done nothing wrong, but the police presence in my rearview gave me a sense of fear. Maybe it was my first encounter with them in the backseat of my mother's car. Perhaps it was the Rodney King beating broadcast to the world a few years earlier. Or maybe it was the innate knowledge of every black male my age that suggested the police meant trouble for me.

Nevertheless, I made the right on Ash Street, not really knowing my destination. All I knew was that I wanted the officer to get off my tail. It never happened. I travelled the main road, passing my turn onto Claiborne Street that would have taken me closer to my parent's house. I continued straight and waited for the police to turn off or go around me in vain.

Then I thought if I made a turn, the police would keep straight. I made a left turn on Leslie Street. As expected the cop followed me on the side road. I pulled to a stop sign at Mulberry Street and that's when the inevitable happened. I saw the blue lights in my rearview mirror.

I didn't move any further. I put the Chevy Nova in park and got my license and registration ready and waited patiently for the officer. I was tired, soaking wet from washing dishes and frustrated at being stopped. I had done nothing wrong and was anxious to see why the officer had pulled me over.

The couple of minutes seemed like an eternity, while bright lights spun in back of me. A female officer finally came to my window and shone a flashlight in my face.

"Let me see your license and registration," she commanded.

I handed her the documents and before I could speak she started interrogating me.

"Is this your vehicle?"

"No ma'am, it's my mother's."

"Where are you coming from tonight?"

"I am just getting off at Texas Steakhouse?"

"Where are you headed?"

"I'm going home," I said, frustrated by the questions. "Why did you stop me for? Did I do something wrong?"

"Just hold tight right here," she stated, ignoring my question. "I'll be right back."

I sat in the car exasperated. I waited about ten minutes for the woman to return. During that period, another police car pulled up. She exited the car and went and spoke to other male officer. After a few minutes, she returned to my window, without handing me back my information.

"Sir, have you had anything to drink tonight," she asked a few inches from my face.

"No! I told you I just got off of work. Look at my clothes and shoes. I'm wet from washing dishes. I just want to go home. I have school tomorrow," I said angrily.

"Well, we're going to have to give you a field sobriety test to see if you've been drinking."

"Look officer, I told you I just got off of work. You see my apron and hat. Why did you stop me in the first place?"

"Well, you didn't come to a complete stop at the light on Spence and Ash, and you were driving suspiciously after that."

"So if I ran the light, why didn't you stop me way back there? Why'd you wait till I got all the way down here," I asked without getting an answer.

"Just step out of the car Mr. Taylor, so we can do the test," the officer insisted.

"I don't know why you are doing this. I'm not drunk. My license and registration are valid. I didn't do nothing wrong. Why don't you just let me go," I protested.

While mumbling under my breath, I exited the car. I left the door open and stood with my teenage arms folded in defiance. The female officer, we'll just call her Officer Moe, started to give me instructions as the male officer etched closer.

"Okay, I am going to hold this pen in the air. Follow the light wherever it goes with your eyes, without moving your head," the lady instructed.

I obeyed the orders and followed the light as she moved it from side to side. Then she moved it up and down and then horizontally again. I passed the test and then braced myself for what was next.

"Alright, now spread your arms out to your side and hold them up. I want you to take your right pointer finger and bring it in slowly and touch the tip of your nose."

I held my head high and performed the task with as much dignity as I could muster. When I did it without error, the officer then commanded me to repeat the process with my left hand. I passed that test as well and waited for the next orders.

"Now, I want you to spread your arms again, and walk in a straight line, putting one foot in front of the other for ten paces. Then turn around and do the same thing coming back."

Like the two previous tests, I completed the feat with no problem. Finding no fault, Officer Moe told me to stand by the car while she and the other officer proceeded to the far vehicle. I watched as they stood there pretending to talk. It then became obvious that they were just stalling as they barely spoke to one another, sneaking glances my way periodically. After a few minutes the woman entered her car, retrieved something from the seat and headed my way again.

"Alright, now we're going to have to give you a breathalyzer test. I need you to blow in this end right here and keep blowing until you here a beep."

"I already passed all the tests," I said defiantly. "I'm just trying to make it home from work. I haven't drunk nothing!" The rage was building up with each second.

"Well, I'm just doing this to make sure. If you just let me do my job, everything will be okay."

Taking the official at her word, I blew my breath in the white tube as hard as I could. Nothing happened. I tried again with more might and finally a beep. The numbers read 0.0.

"See, I told you I haven't been drinking. You know my license are straight, I have no warrants and haven't done anything wrong. Can I please just go home?"

"Just calm down sir, we're almost done. Wait right here for a second," she said nonchalantly.

She once again returned to her partner and did the same song and dance as before. It was obvious that they were just holding me because they could at this point. Even at the tender age of eighteen, I realized this lady was abusing her power and there was nothing I could do.

See, these were the days before cell phones. All I had was a pager. So I was at the mercy of these officers. I had no way to inform my parents, or anyone for that matter, that I was being held, against my will, when I had done nothing wrong.

Just when my frustration and anger was reaching a boiling point, Officer Moe returned with more bad news.

"Just stand right back here. We're going to have to search the vehicle."

"What reason do you have to search my car? All of my information is correct. I'm not drunk. I haven't committed any crime! Why don't you just let me go? This ain't right," I complained uselessly.

"Look, just calm down and be quiet. We're going to search the car to make sure that there are no drugs or weapons in the car," Officer Moe calmly responded.

"I don't have anything," I screamed. "You see I'm just getting off work. I'm in high school! Please let me go!"

The police ignored my pleas and commenced to tear my mother's vehicle apart. They pulled the back seat bottom from the top, rummaged through the trunk, looked under the front seats, rambled through the glove compartment and fiddled in and around the car for about ten minutes. By this time I was furious.

When they were finished, they stood by the driver's side door and did their little pretend conversation routine. I knew they had exhausted all of their reasons for detaining me but they were still stalling. I recognized their tactics and I'd finally had enough.

"Can I go now? Y'all didn't find anything! I'm tired of this! Y'all keep holding me here for nothing! I'm ready to go!"

My words were loud and forceful. I walked toward my car hoping the officers were ready to release me. Evidently the ferocity of my voice is what they were waiting for and they reacted in kind.

"Alright, just calm down. There's no need to get all loud. Everything is gonna be fine," the male officer finally spoke.

"No it's not! Y'all had me out here for about an hour and I gottta go. I'm wet, tired, and sleepy. Just let me go!"

What happened next is sort of a blur. To emphasize my point, I spoke the previous words with my arms flailing in the air and then patting my thighs for impact. My frustration, anxiety and anger had reached the point of explosion.

One of the officers attempted to grab me. I did the natural thing that one does in that instance, which is pull away. I've learned that natural reactions aren't always correct, especially when dealing with law enforcement.

The officers jumped on me simultaneously, trying to get my arms behind my back. I struggled and strived to get loose from their grip, by twisting and turning my body. I spun from right to left and left to right making sure that neither of the officers secured a firm hold on me.

"Stop resisting, stop resisting," they shouted between grunts and gripes as they tried to subdue me.

"No! Get off of me! Let me go! I didn't do nothing," I screamed not letting them get the upper hand.

Finally, I slithered out of their grasps. Disoriented by the sudden escalation, I took off running. I made a left turn on Mulberry and ran into a nearby backyard. When I was out of sight, I ducked into a corner of the house and waited.

The officers had given chase and witnessed the yard that I hid in. With my adrenaline pumping like the blood in my veins, I listened to the footsteps coming up the driveway headed in my direction. As they got closer, I saw the shadow of a person in the twilight. As soon as the figure came into view, I ran past back toward the street.

The officer, Moe, tried to grab me. I shook away from her and ran directly into the path of her partner, who was ready with a can of pepper mace. The spray hit me square in the face and arrested my eyes, nose, mouth and lungs. Confused, dazed, blind and burning I tried to keep running until I had to stop.

That's when I was assaulted. One officer tackled me to the ground. The other put a knee in the spine of my back. I yelped in pain as my arms were twisted in a violent abnormal fashion behind my back. Cuffs were tightly placed around my wrists. Then I was yanked up by the cuffs, causing the hard steel to bore into my skin. I was dragged, pushed and shoved to the police car and thrown forcefully into the back seat.

I was eventually charged with resisting arrest, disorderly conduct and assault on a government official. I was booked, placed in jail, and given a $2,500 dollar bond. I got a chance to call my parents who came to post bail early that morning.

I and my family were embarrassed. My name was listed in the criminal record section of the daily newspaper that next day. I had to attend school with stigma of having been to jail. To the public, I was a common criminal who disobeyed and disrespected the law. In reality, I was just a normal high school student who didn't know how to react while being accosted, harassed and unlawfully detained by antagonistic police officers.

My parents were angry when I told them how things really happened. We called the police station and complained. They even thought about taking an article out in the local paper where my name was slandered. Eventually, like most people who had these types of encounters with police, we accepted the fact that nobody cared or wanted to address the situation.

This experience mirrors so many that happened throughout history and present day America between black men and white police. Officers throughout the land abuse their authority when no one is around to witness or intervene. When these types of situations escalate, they are able to document the events to make the victim look like the aggressor and hold themselves up as the pinnacle of righteousness.

In court, the judges and prosecutors always take the account of the police officers as the unadulterated truth. In my case, I had to return from my freshman year in college to attend court. I was coerced by the local attorney to accept a plea agreement. Being young and naïve, I did. I was convicted and placed on probation, made to pay fines and court costs, and given several hours of community service.

This incident, among others, soured me towards the police. It angered me that someone could stop me at will, detain me at length, search, harass, and assault me without any probable cause. More than that, they did it without retribution. Just like those before me, and those after, black men had no advocate when it comes to the police and the court systems.

This first incident had a tremendous impact on not only my attitude towards police, but also my attitude towards self. I developed a deep disdain and contempt for law enforcement. It was at that point, they became my enemy and I mentally became an outlaw.

In my mind I was stamped; a criminal. If they could do this in my innocence without retribution, then I would make it my destiny to live outside the confines of the law. The predictions of my youth had become true. I had already become a statistic as far as going to jail, so what more did I have to lose.

With this mindset I embarked on a lifestyle that would cause me much grief. I would go on to commit offenses that had the capability of landing me in jail. I take responsibility for these actions and admit I was no angel. However, there were still many instances where I was wrongly targeted, charged, and treated by police. The outcome of these situations may have been different if the deck wasn't already stacked against me, and the scales of justice were equally balanced.

Chapter 11

My First Felony

By the time I graduated high school, I had a record, had sold crack and weed, and drank alcohol and smoked weed on a regular basis. I'd even begun to experiment with the recreational use of powdered cocaine. For all intents in purposes, I had become the prototypical stereotype young black male that America touted. However, as the rule in my household stipulated, I had to go to college after high school; no if, ands, or buts.

I chose North Carolina Central University in Durham, NC, about an hour away. Already engulfed in the street life, leaving Goldsboro was the last thing on my list of things to do. Wanting to continue my criminal enterprise, I embarked on Central's campus with two pounds of marijuana to sell to my fellow students. Since colleges are known for their party atmosphere, I figured I could make good money. I was correct.

I quickly became the man to see for weed. Through my connections to older students from Goldsboro, I became popular and established a large network of customers. I partied, gambled and caroused with girls. It was if I never left home. I took that street mindset with me to college and it caught up with me by the end of the first semester.

In October of 1996, I was set up for a robbery by a student who was from Durham. I was supposed to buy a half-pound of marijuana from his connect. When we got to the location, a man called us behind the building, produced a nine millimeter handgun, and robbed me of my money, jewelry and clothes. He culminated the act by shooting me in the shoulder before commanding me to run away.

This incident once again cemented the idea in my mind that I was a bona fide thug. By the end of my first semester, I no longer went to class. I sat in my dorm room smoking, drinking and selling weed. I saw no future in school and inundated my mind with rap music that glorified and romanticized the life I was living.

At the beginning of the year, I rented a Pathfinder to go to Greensboro for a party at North Carolina A & T University. I, and three friends, took the hour long drive travelling highway 40 east. We had a car full of liquor and I had four ounces of marijuana in a coat in the trunk. Intoxicated out of my mind, I passed a state trooper going 100 mph and got pulled.

The officer was polite and just arrested me without searching the vehicle. I was charged with driving while impaired and reckless driving. I was taken to the precinct, booked, and then released on my own recognizance. One of my friends had license, so he was allowed to drive the vehicle to and from the station.

I include this incident for a reason. This is an example of me clearly committing a crime. That night, I needed to be stopped, lest I hurt myself or someone else. The police officer spotted someone doing wrong and protected and served the community with the utmost professionalism. Had I not been doing wrong, I wouldn't have gotten stopped, so I take full responsibility.

That Monday, after that wild weekend I was back on campus. A friend who lived off site called and asked for a ride to class. I gladly obliged. I took my gun and a bag of weed to smoke on the way back. I had purchased a small .25 caliber pistol after the robbery. I carried it occasionally and this was one morning I decided to.

As I pulled on a street near my friend's house, I encountered a police officer approaching. We looked each other in the eyes when we passed. He immediately turned his car around and hit the sirens. I assume he took one look at the 1997 Pathfinder driven by a young black male and considered it suspicious. This scenario would have been okay with me, if the officer wasn't black also.

When the officer came to the car, he smelled the marijuana smoke from the previous weekend. Also, because of the DWI, my license was instantly revoked. So although he had, nor gave any reason for stopping me, the absence of license and the odor of weed, made the unjust stop justified. He searched the vehicle, found the bag of weed and the pistol.

Instead of taking me to jail, the officer just confiscated the gun and the weed, wrote me a ticket for not having a license and let me go. He instructed me not to drive the jeep, so I walked to my friend's house. He had license, so he drove the jeep back to campus.

This particular stop exemplifies the main point of this book. The only reason I could fathom for the officer stopping me was because of the color of my skin. Also, his keeping of the weed and the gun without charging me is an example of the police misconduct that has been prevalent throughout history. I'm sure that weed was either sold or smoked, and the gun was added to his personal collection.

Because of my actions that first year, my parents refused to send me back to college. For the next three years, I hung around the small town, getting into all sorts of mischief. One summer after leaving work, a simple traffic accident would change my life forever.

By the summer of 1998, I had slipped into the lifestyle I lived before leaving. I had bought a car from a crack addict for a couple of hundred dollars and a few grams of drugs. Despite my activities, I worked overnight at a factory. We worked twelve hours a day, seven days a week, with no breaks. This was certainly against the labor laws. However, I was the only black worker amongst Hispanics and my complaints went unnoticed.

One morning after getting off work, I wanted some weed. At seven o'clock in the morning, there were very little drug dealers standing on corners. I rode around to no avail until I saw some high school students I knew standing at the bus stop. They informed me that they knew a fellow student at school with some.

I piled the three neighborhood children in the car and drove to the school. One went inside while I waited and came out with the drugs. Ironically, the fact that I was able to buy weed from the school is further evidence of the school to prison pipeline.

When we left the school, we headed to a local park where people went to get high. On the way, I was behind a slow moving truck. As he drove slower and slower, I attempted to pass him. Unbeknownst to me, he was slowing for the upcoming stop sign. I ran the sign and slammed smack into a white woman driving a minivan.

We both exited the vehicles and examined the damage. She walked around the car as I apologized and asked was she okay. She said she was and I walked back to assess my totaled car.

When the shock of the accident wore off, I began to think clearly. I remembered I still didn't have any license. Also, I had an open container of beer in the car, a bag of weed, and a few crack rocks for sale in my sock. I realized that when the police arrived, I would be on a fast track to jail, if I didn't do something quick.

I went into the car, grabbed the beer and weed. I then told the high school students, one who already had a broken leg, not to mention my name to the police when they came. I then eased off into a nearby yard and dumped the beer in the trash can. When I noticed the lady wasn't looking, I ran through the backyard, hopped a fence and took off running to a nearby project.

I ended up at the apartment of a high school friend named Kristie. I explained what happened. She agreed to take me home. I thought I was in the clear. However, with a town so small, and three young scary teens, it was just a matter of time before my identity was known.

Later that day, I received calls from the police. They said they knew it was me. Apparently, one of the student's parents was a police officer and they had coerced them to divulge the information. Although they gave them a false name, Ricky Williams, because of my relationship to one of the teens, it was obvious who I was.

At first I denied it. However, after pressure from my parents and the pastor's wife, I agreed to turn myself in. Also, the officer gave me an incentive. He stated that he could charge me with a felony, but if I came down to the precinct voluntarily, it would only be a misdemeanor. Against my better judgement, I agreed.

When I got to the magistrate's office, the policeman was there. He took me into a separate room and sat me down at a table. I watched as he filled out the paperwork. After he finished, he took a paper stamper and pressed down hard on the yellow paper. When he finished, I read the word "felony" in big red letters.

I didn't know the ramifications of that label at that time, so I didn't make a big deal. I did remind him of his promise though. He looked me in the eyes with an evil stare and a slick smirk, walked out of the room and handed the warrant to the magistrate.

I was booked on the charges and given a $5000 dollar bond. Fortunately, I had the money from working to post bail. It would be more than a year before I went to court. The results of the case will be discussed in the next chapter.

However, while awaiting the disposition of the case, I did some research. My mother was upset about the possibility of me having a felony on my record. Being that she worked for the Federal

Bureau of Prisons, she knew how much a felony could affect my future.

After looking up the statutes on the difference between felony and misdemeanor hit and run, I knew I had been had. The only requirement for the felony was that the person I hit had to be injured. The way that lady got out of the car and walked around, she was in no way hurt. At worst, I should have only been charged with misdemeanor hit and run; at best, leaving the scene of an accident. This situation is a prime example how police officers can manipulate and exacerbate charges on their own whim.

In this officer's case, he was just being evil. In fact, for the next twelve years, he continued to stop and harass me without cause. In one instance, I wasn't even staying in Goldsboro any longer. It was seven years later when I came to visit that I encountered him again.

I was visiting my father, who was delivering mail on his route in a local housing project. While leaving my father, I passed the officer as he was entering the project. When I noticed him, I blew my horn when we caught each other's eye. I wanted him to see the Real Estate signs with my name on the side of my car. I had just endured a four month long process with Virginia's Real Estate Commission to obtain my license. They initially denied me because of the only felony on my record, unnecessarily charged by the same officer.

He immediately turned around and got behind me. He waited until I was a mile down the road to pull me over. I asked for the reason after he verified my license and registration. He gave no excuse as I reminded him who I was.

"Do you remember me? I'm Richard Taylor! You gave me a felony seven years ago for a hit and run after you said you wouldn't! But look at me now. I'm a license real estate agent. Even though you gave me that felony I still succeeded. And look at you, still on patrol."

The man took offense to my statements. I didn't mean any harm at first. The more I thought about the struggle I had to get licensed just a couple of weeks before, led to frustration. Evidently he was irritated too.

"Get out of the car Mr. Taylor."

"No, I'm not. For what, I didn't do anything wrong."

He responded by pulling my door open and motioning me out. I complied but got angry at his next command.

"Turn around and put your hands behind your back."

I again obeyed as he clamped handcuffs around my wrists. I started giving him some choice words. I knew I hadn't committed an offense and I felt justified in letting him know how I felt. He ran my information while I grew impatient.

In the midst of this exchange, my father drove by in his mail truck and noticed me standing in handcuffs. He pulled over and asked, what was the problem? I explained the situation and he was just as irritated as I.

"Well, why do you have him in handcuffs like that? There's no need for that."

The officer waved my dad off. He finally came back to my car, took the cuffs off and handed my license back. He also gave me a ticket for having tints that were too dark. After not being able to find anything to charge me with, he had to come up with something.

I accepted the ticket with grace. Before I drove off, I got out of my car, walked up to the cruiser and gave him my business card.

"If you ever know anyone that could use my help, give me a call."

He took the card with a smirk. This was another occasion where the officer stopped me for no reason at all. However, being that he was an officer of the law, and the courts believed their reports beyond a shadow of a doubt, he could easily come up with some violation to justify his actions.

This same officer would repeat the scenario five years later when I moved back to Goldsboro. He saw me driving and immediately made a U-turn.

This time, I panicked, turned into a friend's yard and brushed up against the vinyl siding on the house. As I did twelve years earlier, I left the scene. As a result, I was charged with a few misdemeanors. My friend refused to pursue charges since there was no damage to his house. However, the officer gave me as many charges as he could to ensure I was convicted of something.

Later that month, he stopped me again while I was transporting residents from a group home I worked at. He said he stopped me because he thought I didn't have a license. When I produced the terms of a provisional driver's permit, he had to let me go.

However, a few days later, I received a call from the clerk to return to court. Evidently, the officer went to the courts, looked at my paperwork and found a way to have my provisional license revoked. This is a prime example of an officer having a vendetta and abusing his position of authority to enforce it. I would later find out why.

After speaking to one of the officer's partners, I found out that he was going through a domestic situation. His wife had left him and was having an affair with a black man. Just this fact alone, given his position, gave him the opportunity to take his frustration out on the many black men he encountered on a daily basis.

In addition, this officer has since become a sergeant or detective from what I know. One doesn't ascend to higher positions unless he has proven himself worthy by making numerous arrests. The direct correlation between substantiating charges and advancement is a conflict of interest as it relates to justice.

This officer is just one of many who let their personal biases, situations and aspirations interfere with the professional and equitable performance of their jobs. This is a problem throughout America. Men and women, who are flawed, are allowed to pursue the mistakes of others. Driven by personal interests or grudges, they can use their influence to highlight the flaws of others.

The police officers are here to protect and serve. However, the modern day police have been made to target the same people that they vow to protect. Truly, they only protect the status quo and serve the interests of a government that has shown to be indifferent, intolerable, and unjust to a large population of the country. I am just one of many who have been affected by this targeting and the lifelong label and stigma of being a felon.

Chapter 12

Prison Time

During the five year period between 1997 and 2002, the year I finally left Goldsboro, I got into a lot of trouble. In that time, I amassed charges ranging from possession of marijuana, D.W.I's (3), driving while license revoked, trespassing, assaults, to carrying a concealed weapon, possession of a stolen firearm, common law robbery and armed robbery amongst others. Time or space will not permit to delve into each instance. I will be first to admit, in most of these cases I contributed to the occurrences.

However, sometimes searches were still unwarranted. Once, while playing cards in a poolroom, officers came to the door. The owner, an elder gentleman named Willie Simmons, allowed them in. The one officer, a black man who went to the same high school I attended, came straight to me. He searched me, and found the .357 magnum I had in my waistband. The charge of carrying a concealed weapon was upgraded at the magistrate's office when it was uncovered that the gun was stolen.

While again, it was wrong for me to have the gun. But this officer's actions were another result of a longstanding grudge against me. His girlfriend at the time, stayed next door to a store we hustled at. One day, he pulled up to her house and saw us talking. Ever since that day, whether I was driving, walking, or stationary, he would accost me on sight.

The same officer would arrest me for a second driving while impaired offense. In the latter part of 1998, I was driving a vehicle to see a female who stayed in a project area. As I turned into the entrance, he was exiting. As we passed, he looked into the car, noticed it was me, and turned immediately around.

Since I was driving on a suspended license, I attempted to get away. I speedily turned the next corner, and the next, and parked in front of my friend's house. I hopped out of the car, ran to her door and knocked hard. Once she didn't answer, I ran around back to some nearby woods behind the apartments.

I hid in the woods for about an hour. I heard police searching the area and canvassing with dogs like I had killed the president. After I thought they left, I climbed from my hiding place, only to find the officers standing a few yards away. I was arrested and transported to the local jail.

I was given a variety of charges. For the two bottles of Myer's Jamaican Rum and Seagram's Gin, they charged me with transporting spirituous liquors. Driving while license revoked, resisting arrest, and driving while impaired were also added to the list. To make matters worse, the car was impounded, not to be released pending the disposition of the case.

Again I admit that I shouldn't have owned or been driving the vehicle under the influence or with alcohol in the car. However, without him targeting and knowing me from so many instances, I would have never been caught. There are so many cases like this that could be disputed and defeated because of unlawful stops. Defendants are rarely given the option to choose that defense.

Fast forward to April, 1999, I sat in a Goldsboro jail cell for another minor offense. I was awaiting bail that had not come the night before. The next morning, I was scheduled for a court appearance for the above mentioned DWI. My intention was to get a continuance, but my court appointed lawyer had other plans.

We got to court and this was the first time I had seen the man since the arraignment five months earlier. We hadn't discussed any possibilities or outcomes. When I was escorted into the courtroom chained to other inmates, the black lawyer came with a vague discussion of the upcoming scenario.

"Hey Taylor, you wanna go ahead and get this thing over with today?"

"Well, I was gonna ask for a continuance. I don't want to go before the judge in this orange jumpsuit. I need more time," I countered.

"I mean, if that's what you want to do, that's fine. But this is a good judge."

"I thought the law mandated a year on the second DWI. I'm not ready to go to jail for a year today," I insisted.

"No you're not gonna get a year. You'll probably get 30 to 45 days, tops. We'll just see what happens."

With that, he turned and went to talk to some other detainees. Everything in my heart told me to go with my original plans. My mind however, considered the logic of the lawyer. I could do thirty days as opposed to a year. Even though I was getting bonded later that day, I decided to plead guilty, which was a mistake.

The judge called my case and I stood before him in leg chains and handcuffs. The lawyer gave a few inaudible statements about me and the situation before entering a plea of guilty. When asked did I want to speak, he advised me not to.

The judge pronounced me guilty and immediately imposed a sentence of 12 months in the North Carolina Department of Corrections. I looked at the court appointed lawyer with surprise. He gave me a stoic glare of indifference as the bailiff led me away to a holding cell. Once I returned to the jail, I got on my bunk and cried silently.

The next day I was shipped to the Neuse Correctional facility, a misdemeanor camp on the outskirts of Goldsboro. As soon as I processed and made it to the dormitory, I saw several people I knew from the streets. I was held in a processing dorm for three days, before I was released to regular population.

Because this was a camp where prisoners were on their last leg of long term sentences, or sentenced to misdemeanors like me, the atmosphere was laid back. I soon fell into the routine of lifting weights, playing ball, or gambling. I even went to the library during recreational time.

A few older guys from Goldsboro took me under their wing and gave me the dos and don'ts of prison life. There was a structure; a hierarchy of sorts. Only certain people were allowed to run card games, football pools, and loan shark. I found out this the hard way as I was running a poker game that was shut down by the poker man one day.

About a month in I was assigned to the kitchen. We had to get up at about three or four and head to the cafeteria to prepare breakfast. I was placed in the pantry and had to gather all the ingredients on the cart for the cooks. I was mostly by myself all day as I had to repeat the same task for lunch.

I enjoyed this position because I had a lot of free time to read or write. I also had unlimited access to the food supply. I would snack all day and drink the ensure protein shakes like water. This lasted for a minute until I was moved to dishwasher. That was a much more strenuous position, but I did get to laugh, joke, and have more camaraderie with the other men.

It was then that I saw how a man could get used to prison. Many of my peers from Goldsboro, and the ones I met there, had already done several separate stretches. They were accustomed to the life. As long as they got visits, canteen, money, telephone calls, cards, weights and board games, they were straight. Not to mention the weed, alcohol and other drugs that entered the facility.

Yes, the prison system isn't immune to the drug epidemic. The drugs were sometimes brought in by guards. Other times they could be smuggled in through visits. Sometimes the guys that were on the road squad, who cleaned up the highways, would have someone leave packages at predetermined locations to be picked up later. Nevertheless, there was never a shortage of marijuana when I was there. I even smoked a few times myself.

The first few months changed my view of prison. There were no gang rapes, no violent riots, stabbings or murders. Most conflicts were over minor things like cards or the television control.

Most of the inmates were civilized, career criminals who were on their way home.

In July, things changed. I was scheduled to attend court for the hit and run felony charge from the previous year. On that date, I was roused early, fed, and transported by sheriff from the prison to the courthouse.

I was nervous. I wanted to continue the case. Just like before, I didn't want to appear before a judge already in the custody of the state. As I experienced, things are less favorable when the defendant already appears to be an inmate.

Also, from the court appointed lawyer, who I won't name, I was told the charge would carry a sentence of fifteen months. I definitely didn't want to do that time. So, my intentions were to fight the case.

When I arrived at the court, I spoke to my lawyer about pleading not guilty. He said that I should plead guilty. I explained that the lady wasn't hurt, which is the basis for the felony charge. He countered that she was present and ready to testify of her injuries. When I entered the courtroom, I saw the stout white lady, along with my mother and the arresting officer in the pews.

I was chained with other prisoners on the first row of the court. The court appointed lawyer came and told me that he would try to get a plea agreement. When my case was called, I moved to sit at the desk beside the lawyer. He whispered into my ear.

"They've offered a plea of four to five months. Since you still have three months left on your current sentence, you'll only have to do an extra month. They're going to run it concurrent with the sentence you have."

"So, you mean the four months would start today," I clarified.

"That's correct. I think it's a good deal."

"But I don't want the felony. That's the thing. I mean, she wasn't hurt. I don't want that on my record."

"I understand. She's here and she is going to say that she was hurt. We can fight it, but you're looking at another fifteen months to two years instead of getting out of prison in a few months. It's up to you."

Presented with that scenario, I took the deal. It made sense. I could get this case over with and still not face any substantial amount of extra time. I had already adjusted to prison, so what was one extra month.

Although I agreed, this is an example of a major problem with the judicial system and its players. This lawyer's job was clearly to dispose of the case with a plea agreement. The prosecutor's objective was to give the most favorable offer in order to secure a conviction. The judge's job was to adhere to the proposition of both attorneys in order to lighten the court's docket.

The only one who loses is the defendant. No one is in search for justice, just disposition. In my case, I was encouraged by my representation to take an agreement that would benefit my immediate situation, but would affect my entire life with the labeling of a felon. I may have been able to avoid this, if not for the professional prodding of my advocate.

This advocate, by the way, was very instrumental in handling the cases of many others in like manner over the years. Most of the cases ended in plea agreements. His name was a constant on the court calendar for all types of offenses.

However, this lawyer was also involved in drug usage for years. It had been rumored and I've had people tell me that they paid for their services with drugs. This suspicion was confirmed years later, when he was caught with cocaine in his possession on more than one occasion in a neighboring city. So in essence, this same court official had sent several people to jail or prison, for the same or lesser offenses than he committed. In a recent trip to the courthouse, I saw this same lawyer, still practicing law after being charged with criminal behavior.

The same applies to judges and police officers. There was a prominent judge who was caught taking bribes and doing other nefarious things. He was charged and convicted, but not sent to jail. He has since started another career and is still flourishing. While sentencing others to long terms, he broke laws that he took an oath to uphold.

There is a double standard that exists when those who should be held to higher standards are granted leniency because of their positions in the legal system. Meanwhile, those who are judged by the transgressors of the law have no recourse.

Nevertheless, I was sentenced on the felony charge and was transferred from the Neuse prison to the James K. Polk youth facility in Raleigh. Even though I was 21, I was still considered ineligible for the adult system. I was in for a rude awakening upon my arrival at Polk.

At the Neuse, the population was about 75% black. At Polk, however, the ratio was at least 90% black. Young men from the age of 18 to 21 were confined with sentences of 10, 20, 25, 42, and even 63 years. So the atmosphere was very aggressive as many of the prisoners had nothing to lose and everything to gain by establishing themselves violently.

I had no fear. Just like the Neuse, as soon as I entered the dorm, I heard someone call my name. It was a childhood friend who had been there for over a year. He quickly informed me that there were more than twenty inmates from Goldsboro at Polk.

A few had been there for years and were established in the system. We had little to worry about.

The most deplorable thing about the prison was the conditions. We were on what was considered the "old side." There were several pods that had bunks upstairs and downstairs with a dayroom on the bottom and showers on top. There were 60 or so people to a pod and four pods to a dorm. It was very tight and tensions constantly arose.

I arrived in the middle of July, the dead of summer. The dorms were outdated and had no air-condition system. We suffered through hot days and nights, drenched in sweat. With little to no ventilation, the only reprieve was the industrial fans that circulated the hot air, and the daily trips to the rec yard. The heat of the sun was not much better.

Eventually, I got used to the routine. I started playing chess, lifting weights, playing basketball and gambling at cards. I made alliances, connections, and formed bonds, trying to avoid the conflicts that were so prevalent. Despite my efforts, the inevitable eventually occurred.

One day we were on the rec yard. I came back to the dorm and someone had broken into my locker. I made a fuss about it, calling whoever did it names and talking about their mother. I eventually stretched on my bunk and put my headphones in.

Apparently the insults got to the culprit. I felt cold, soapy water hit my face while at the same time a long, brown skinned arm swung a punch. I hopped off the top bunk and we began fighting. The guards came in and broke it up. Since he was the aggressor, he was removed from the dorm. After an investigation, he was deemed to be at fault. He was sentenced to the hole, while I received no punishment.

The next couple of days while on the yard, I was told that his partners were angry for what happened. They sent word that they were going to do something to me. Trying to avoid another conflict, I informed the guards. They did nothing. I told some of my peers from Goldsboro and they vowed to watch my back.

The next day around rec time, I was alone. My partners had medical appointments and court. I knew I would have to face the man's two friends when I went to the yard. I walked through the outside doors reluctantly as the two chiseled youth awaited.

As I walked passed them, I was immediately struck in the back of the head. I realized that the punch didn't hurt. So I turned around and went toe to toe with the guy who hit me. The fear was gone and I was handling myself fairly well.

Out of the corner of my eye, I noticed his friend coming toward me. Without warning, I disengaged and caught the oncoming fighter with a right to the jaw. We started squabbling until the guards came and broke it up. I felt good about myself, having confronted the threat and came out unscathed.

Once again, I was spared punishment because it was two against one. The two were given a gang charge for jumping me and sent to the hole for twenty one days. Afterwards, I gained respect from my peers and had no more problems, except for a couple of minor disagreements with people from my hometown.

The only other problems I experienced were with the correctional officers. Like the inmates, most of them were black also. However, they treated us like we were less than animals. The way they talked to us was dehumanizing and demeaning.

One sergeant, an old black man, spoke real dirty to me while I was being released. I addressed his tone and demeanor and gave him the same energy. He became even more belligerent.

"You better shut up, before I put a charge on you and you won't be going nowhere!"

"That's sad man. You just want somebody to be locked up in here with you. I was here for four months. You've been here for twenty something years. You're institutionalized," I countered.

"Oh, don't worry about it. You'll be back. You know what you are? You're just job security to me. You just a stupid little nigger. You'll be back."

"You're pitiful," I responded. "You're just old and bitter. You gonna spend your life behind these bars!"

"Say one more word! You ain't gonna have to worry about getting out. I'm gonna jump on your ass and nobody in here is gonna stop me. Just try me!"

With that, I just shook my head and continued through the process. It amazed me then and still now how people can operate a system with such vigor knowing that it is stacked against them and those who look like them. This was my first and last prison experience, but not my last encounter with officers or law enforcement officials that operate from a personal disdain for those in their control. I will never forget that exchange.

Chapter 13

Corruption

After release from prison, I returned to Goldsboro. A newly branded felon, the transition was hard. Even though I had a good support system, the experience of confinement had scarred me for life. I tried to enroll in school, secure and maintain a job but soon fell back into the lifestyle that landed me in trouble. This chapter will focus on some of the experiences I witnessed and endured in my hometown since the year 2000.

The first incident of police brutality actually happened before my incarceration. I was falsely accused of robbery by an acquaintance after a dispute over a card game. I suspected a player of cheating and in turn reached over the table and took my money back. When he stood up to protest, I pulled a pistol and he retreated.

By the time I arrived at my parent's house, the police were there. I dodged them that morning, but the next day, they caught me asleep in bed. I was arrested and charged with robbery with a dangerous weapon. The man had fabricated a story of me coming to his house and asking to borrow one hundred dollars. He said when he refused I pulled a gun and robbed him of six hundred dollars and a gold chain.

When I got to the precinct and heard this version of events I was livid. Throughout the interrogation, I told both detectives the story was a lie. However, as I would experience many times in the future, the word of an accuser was believed without doubt. I was booked on the charges and given a hundred thousand dollar bond.

While being escorted downstairs to the holding cells, I proceeded to insult the two detectives in my anger. As usual, the officers injected their own form of trash talk while handling me roughly in transport.

The situation came to a head when we reached the cell. I was so upset about not being able to get out my fury rose to madness. The officers weren't far away as we went back and forth.

When the cuffs were removed and I was placed in the cell, I gave a few more insults and launched a glob of spit in the officer's direction. I'm not sure if it made contact but the reaction of the two men was swift.

They entered the cell with stealth and began pummeling me with blows to my face, neck and chest. I didn't swing back because I knew the legal and physical ramifications would only get worse. So I endured the assault, which wasn't so bad, due to the age and unfitness of the elderly white men. The affray ended when one detective had to beg, plead and literally pull his partner off of me. The anger was evidenced in the face of both men as their skin tone was beet red.

Later that day, I received about five more charges; two of which were assault on a government official. The assault was me spitting on one of their ties. There was no mention of the beating they inflicted upon me. Once again, the double standard emerged. Even though I was wrong and take full responsibility for spitting, the officers still acted unprofessionally and criminally in the way they assaulted me. I even attempted to press charges on them to no avail.

I stayed in jail about 45 days awaiting a reduction in bail. I endured the same demeaning treatment from the black and white sheriff deputies. Eventually, I was released and the charges of robbery were dropped a year later when the witness failed to show up for court. Nevertheless, I had to still plead guilty for the other charges and received a two year probation sentence. This could have been avoided if the police would have done due diligence and never arrested me on the false charges to begin with.

For the next couple of years I would have other strange encounters with the police. Once, another associate called the police on me and a close friend. We had a disagreement days earlier and it had not been resolved. Both I and my friend had guns when the man spotted us at a local convenience store. We circled around and pulled into the lot. A few seconds later the police pulled up behind us.

The officer, who knew us, asked to search the vehicle. I was a passenger and had placed my pistol under the seat. The driver had done the same. We got out of the car when my friend gave consent.

The officer wasted no time in finding the weaponry. To our surprise, he confiscated the guns and told us to go on our way. Even though I was grateful, in legal terms, the search was unlawful. Also, I wondered what the officer did with those guns. He couldn't have turned them in without related charges.

This officer, who was black, represents how police should operate. He used discretion because he knew us. He knew our families and our upbringing. However, he removed items that shouldn't have been in our possession, without putting a further blemish on our records.

Another officer, a female, demonstrated the same restraint. She once saw me driving and from past experiences, knew I wasn't licensed. She got behind me and I pulled into the nearest parking lot in a housing project. I exited the car and attempted to walk away, but she called my name. I had to stop.

I turned around and returned to the car. She asked me a rhetorical question about my license and I stated that I had none. She then proceeded to search the vehicle and discovered about two hundred dollars-worth of marijuana bagged in nickel and dime bags. I was caught red handed and expected jail.

However, like the other officer, she just took the drugs and told me not to drive off in her presence. This officer stayed less than two blocks from my parents and knew them personally. So even though I was wrong, the stop was illegal, and the officer gave me leniency, I was still a victim of targeting. To this day, I still wonder what the officer did with that weed. Being that her lips were black and her own son smoked weed and had been in trouble, I doubt that the drugs ever made it to the evidence room.

Another occasion I was standing in my aunt's yard with a few of my cohorts. I, my cousins and their friends used the location to sell marijuana and other drugs. On this day, we were all standing by the side of the road when the Aggressive Crime Enforcement unit, or the jump out boys, rounded the corner heading directly toward us.

Nobody made a move. However, I remembered that I had an eighth of an ounce, or an eight ball, of crack in my pocket, along with a quarter ounce of weed. I took off running towards the house as officer Stapps hopped out of the vehicle and gave chase.

Knowing I couldn't get into the house, I had to think fast. I reached in my pocket while running and pulled out the crack. I placed the small plastic bag in my mouth just as I was tackled from behind. Before the officer placed his hands around my neck, I was able to swallow the drugs to avoid a felony possession charge. I then endured the customary beating that accompanied any attempt to flee from the law.

I was searched and charged with the quarter ounce of marijuana. I went to jail, was given a miniscule bond and made bail. Less than a couple of hours later, I was back on the same corner.

This tactic is the example of the targeting discussed in earlier chapters. Even though I was in possession of illegal substances, the officers had no legal justification. The only reason was that I was a black man in a black neighborhood.

I harp on this because there are several other neighborhoods where drug use and distribution is prevalent. Affluent sections of the town like Walnut Creek, Lane Tree, and Country Day Road all are filled with teens and adults who use drugs. The only difference is that road blocks, and raids are not set up in that area of town to catch users and dealers. If by chance they are, the offenders have mothers, fathers, aunts, uncles, or grandparents who work in the system and are able to sweep the situation under the proverbial legal rug.

This double standard exists on a higher scale. I am reminded of a well-known incident where a judge, a prominent businessman, and a pastor were caught on a boat with a large amount of cocaine. However, because of their positions, nothing ever came of the case. The judge kept judging, the businessman kept selling and the preacher kept preaching.

There was another case where nearly 100 kilos of cocaine were found on the property of another well to do power broker of the city. Instead of the property owner facing charges, an employee of his who ran a local store took the rap. Even so, he was only sentenced to two years.

So the imbalance is clear. You have young black offenders spending years in prison for having an ounce or two of cocaine or crack. Yet you have powerful white men who transport millions of dollars in drugs and get off scot free or with a slap on the wrist. This shouldn't be so.

In 2003 I left Goldsboro, and moved to Virginia. After six years, and many other experiences, which I will address later, I moved back. I would soon find out that little had changed in that time period.

Upon my return, I initially stayed away from illegal activities. I worked for a group home where I transported residents to and from appointments. It was on this occasion that I was harassed by the officer who had charged me with the hit and run ten years earlier. He disputed my request for a provisional license and caused me to attend court to reapply.

On this court date, I entered the hallway of the courtroom and was confronted by a bailiff. I knew him from before. He always threw his weight around. He wasn't letting people enter for some reason. When I said something about the time and not wanting to miss roll call, he acted if it wasn't a big deal.

I then went to the clerk of court in the next hallway over. I informed her of my presence there and my inability to enter the courtroom. While leaving the office, I noticed four deputies manhandling a man in civilian clothes. Apparently they were arresting him for some reason. He held his body sturdy while the four white men struggled to move him.

Because I knew the man, resentment for the officers grew in my belly. When I reached the hallway by the courtroom entrance, I was again stopped by the bailiff. We exchanged words again and he said something to the effect of me not being able to enter if I didn't shut up. I informed him that he couldn't prevent me from entering. After another exchange, he informed me that I was being arrested for contempt of court.

I protested lightly as the bailiff put handcuffs on me and placed me in a cell in the rear of the courtroom. The cell had a small window. I peeked out and waited to be transported to the magistrate.

While looking through the glass, I saw the same man that deputies had subdued in the clerk's hallway. They were still dragging and pulling him in different directions as he was handcuffed. He still talked trash and held his body firm, defiantly against the officers' aggression.

Out of nowhere, an older officer began punching and striking the man in the face and chest. The man took the punches while still hurling insults at his attackers. Then, a different officer took out a TASER and struck the man with the electric current. He hit the floor under the influence.

Upon recovering, he still spoke and berated the officers. He belittled them saying that it was four on one and that he could handle the TASER as well

This didn't sit well with the officers as they started to beat him again. When he withstood the onslaught, they used the TASER again, but much longer. The man screamed and yelled until the current subsided. Due to the severity, the officers had to pull the needles from the gun out of the man's arm. The man was defenseless in handcuffs. His only offense was talking junk to the officers.

As soon as I was released on a minor bail, I exposed what happened to me and what I saw. I took to social media and ranted. I composed a detailed letter of the events from start to finish. I sent the document certified to the mayor, chief of police, clerk's office, head sheriff, the local newspaper, and had more copies reserved for other entities if I didn't get results.

A week before I was to attend court, I received a call from the sheriff stating that he wanted to speak with me. When I arrived, I spoke to the acting sheriff, a black man, because the main sheriff was sick. I sat down not knowing what to expect.

I listened as he told me how disturbing the letters were and how they needed to stop. He informed me if I dropped my complaints against the courts and sheriff's office, then he would also dismiss the pending charges against me. Reluctantly, I agreed.

I did not want to cease my pursuit of justice, but I felt it had accomplished something. I knew if I didn't, then they would stick it to me in court. Also, I knew, just like today, the court would never go against the grain and punish their officials.

In essence, this situation reminds me of Breonna Taylor and her boyfriend's situation. To cover up the fact that they went into her house with reckless abandon and riddled her body with bullets, they charged the boyfriend with firing at them. Then in order to keep him silent, they agreed to drop the charges as long as he wouldn't speak on the situation. This is on a much larger scale, but as proved in my case, it happens in cities all across the country, where people have no voice or advocacy.

Nevertheless, I stayed around my hometown. I eventually grew discouraged and began using alcohol and drugs again. I started hanging around old friends and associates, getting high on a regular basis. One such circle was frequented by member of law enforcement, who sniffed cocaine and drunk with us.

I used to listen to stories how he and his white counterparts loved when a suspect would resist or run. He bragged about how they beat them with impunity. Even if the subject was incoherent, incapacitated or mentally ill, it didn't matter. It was a mob mentality that overtook the officials and they thought it okay.

Around that time, a man was killed by members of city's law enforcement. They were called to the scene of a fight. When they arrived, there was no evidence of a fight, just an intoxicated man sitting on a porch.

From media accounts, they tried to escort the man home. In the process, a TASER was used.

According to reports, this was the cause of death. The man had a previous heart condition and the use of the gun allegedly sent him into cardiac arrest. The family of the decease blamed police for the use of the electric gun, knowing that he had health problems from previous contact.

However, I received a different version of events. Days later, at our usual drinking and drugging spot, the law enforcement officer attended. He explained how he was called to the scene and the guy tried to run. He relayed how he and other officers jumped on the man and beat him. When he wouldn't stop moving they beat him and stunned him until he lay lifeless on the ground.

From the look in his eye and the passion in his voice I knew it was true. I could see how the officers got lost in the moment just by listening to him retell the story. He justified his actions by saying the guy shouldn't have ran and resisted. The sad thing is both the officer and the victim were black. He put his loyalty to his position over his responsibility to humanity and engaged in acts with others that caused the death of one of his own.

I stayed around Goldsboro for about a year until 2011. Then I moved back to Virginia. My first week back, I had a near death experience with the Virginia Beach Sheriff Department, on which I'll expound upon in the next chapter. After a short stint in the county jail, I decided to get my life together and make a difference.

I enrolled in Tidewater Community College in Norfolk, VA. I restarted the book that became my first novel, "Brushes with Death," published in 2012. I also began studying social issues and became active in problems plaguing the black community in Goldsboro and Norfolk.

In the summer of 2012 I grew increasingly concerned with the affairs in my hometown. There was in upsurge of violence including several unsolved murders in the low income areas of the city. From appearances, the city's government and law enforcement were content with the state of affairs. I even got some reports that police and officials were complicit and instrumental in ensuring that the violence continued.

I started to galvanize the people of the community in an effort to address city officials. I passed out fliers, called forums, and organized neighborhood groups and representatives to speak on their concerns. I even started to dig into the city's budget and mismanagement of funds supposedly designated for low income areas. I travelled from Virginia to Goldsboro several times to stay involved.

On one such visit I was passing out fliers to encourage people to come out to a meeting I'd set up with the mayor, city manager, police chief and other officials. The paper highlighted issues in the community that were being neglected. I placed them on convenient store windows, places of business, and various locations throughout the city. I even placed one over a campaign sign in the current mayor's yard only a few blocks from my parents.

The night before the meeting I was walking in the neighborhood after posting the fliers. A block from my parent's house I was stopped by the same lady police officer who'd took the weed from me years earlier. She rolled up on me like a scene from "In the Heat of the Night."

"Hey, how are you doing tonight," she asked.

"I'm alright. What's going on," I replied.

"Nothing, what are you doing out here?"

"I'm heading home. You know I stay around the corner."

"Yeah, I know. Where are you coming from," she continued to prod.

"I was out passing out fliers for the meeting tomorrow with the mayor."

"Oh, so you're the one who has been passing out those fliers." The way her eyes enlarged at my statement, made me aware that I'd upset someone by my actions. I felt the tension and presence of a threat in the air.

"Yeah, that's me. You know who I am. Don't you remember me?"

"Yeah, I know who you are," she answered with a sideways look. "What's in the bag?"

"Just some paperwork; is there a problem or something officer," I inquired.

"No, not at all, do you want a bottle of water?"

"No, I'm good. Are we done here?"

"Yeah, are you sure you don't want a bottle of water. It's mighty hot out here."

"I'm fine," I said with a smirk, and started walking off.

"Alright now," she said as she rode slowly beside me. "You be careful out here."

I looked at her to as if to say "what are you talking about." By her demeanor, I knew exactly what she meant.

"Alright," I said trying to get out of her presence quickly.

"You should take a bottle of water before I go," she implored again.

"I'm straight. Have a good night though."

She finally drove away but not before admonishing to be careful again. There was an eerie feeling; a sense of alarm. I felt like a freedom fighter in the sixties, after being stopped by an officer in rural Mississippi. I interpreted her warnings to be careful as an indirect threat and couldn't wait to cross the threshold of my parent's door.

Long story short, I had the meeting the next day. It was futile. The leaders ignored the points outlined in my presentation. I ended up storming out of the meeting when the answers to my questions were laced with political double talk. I went back to Virginia and continued my schooling, writing, and social activism from a distance.

I thought nothing more of the encounter with the officer the night before the meeting. About two or three months later, I received a call from one of my classmates. He told me that his mother worked inside City Hall and had heard my name come up in conversation with city leaders.

"My mom asked me did I still talk to you. She wanted me to give you a call," he explained.

"Your mom," I clarified. "What's going on?"

"Well, she told me to tell you that you might want to be careful with what you're doing around Goldsboro," he continued.

"What you mean? Why would she say that?"

"You know she works down at City Hall. She's been there for some years now. She said that she overheard some people talking about you and thought you should know," my friend informed.

"So what were they talking about? What did they say?"

"She said that they said they are going to have to shut you up. And they were serious. So she told me to tell you to be careful."

I knew he was telling the truth. I had been going so hard exposing the leadership and their money mishandling that they could not let me continue. I took the warning to heart, as I thought about the encounter a couple of months earlier.

However, I continued to work less vocally and visibly behind the scenes with various organizations and initiatives. People would still call me from Goldsboro and tell me about their incidents with police and the nefarious things that happened in the city.

Around the same time, another situation occurred that garnered my attention. In August of that year, my cousin was involved in a botched drug raid that left one man dead and my cousin facing five counts of attempted murder of police. Another cousin of mines was shot in the foot, probably by a bullet fired by police.

The official story was that the police went to the house to serve a drug warrant. When they busted down the door, they claimed someone opened fire. In response, the officers returned fire, riddling the space with bullets, killing a Jamaican immigrant and wounding one cousin. The other cousin was charged with firing the weapon and jailed without bond.

I took the city's version of events at face value initially. However, I later received a call from a female classmate regarding the case. She was the girlfriend of the deceased and stated that she had something to show me. We set up a date when I would be back in North Carolina.

At the meeting, we sat at the kitchen table of my parent's house. She produced a DVD provided to her by the late boyfriend's lawyer. The contents shocked me and let me know that there was much more to what happened on the night of the man's demise.

On the video, the Jamaican man was being stopped and detained by two sheriff deputies. The screen showed the back of his car with the trunk open. One officer spoke with the man while the other sat in the vehicle, conversing with a confidential informant in the back seat.

"That's him isn't it? You said it was in the trunk right," the officer asked the snitch.

"Yeah, everything was just like I said; even the street he was gonna be travelling."

The officer and the informant continued speaking. It was evident that the person knew exactly what the man would have, when he would have it, and where he would be. The other officer came back to the car and left the man standing by the trunk in cuffs.

"Well, he's got a garbage bag full of marijuana in that trunk. I smelled it when I pulled him over," the driver said with a southern twang.

"She was right," his partner responded. "So what do you want to do?"

"Let's see. We can take the marijuana, and let him go like nothing ever happen."

"Or, we can just shoot him and act like he tried to run," the partner countered.

"Or maybe just kill him and take the weed."

I watched in awe as two law enforcement officials talked openly about killing this man as if they were discussing what to eat for dinner. Their maliciousness aside, the officers eventually merely arrested the man. However, a year after the stop, and a short time before his death, the accused would beat the charges with a technicality found by his lawyer.

I was furious, scared and excited all at the same time. I pleaded with my friend to let me get the disk or at least make me a copy. I couldn't wait to show it to the news media, lawyers, senators, the governor, justice advocates, or anyone who cared to see. Unfortunately, or maybe fortunately for my and her safety, she refused to part with the damning evidence.

I felt the video proved there was more to what happened on the night of her boyfriend's death. Just the officer's words and the fact that he beat the investigation against him, was more than proof that the officers had a vendetta and a reason to go into that house with guns blazing. Furthermore, I felt the video would be instrumental in setting my cousin free.

Nevertheless, my cousin sat in jail for nearly three years fighting the charges. All of sudden, the case was dropped; no conviction, no explanation, nothing. That gives further credence to my theory of police misconduct. They made him sit in jail under the threat of life in prison, so he couldn't tell what really happened. After all of the hoopla died down, they let him out. In the many times I've seen him since, he has yet to mention that night.

The instances in this chapter exhibit the capacity for criminal intent of those in law enforcement, political or judicial positions. Whether judges, prosecutors, attorneys, city officials, police officers or sheriffs, all of them are subject to human flaw. They possess the ability for hatred, lust, greed, prejudice, bitterness, anger, spite, vengeance and to be influenced by stereotypes.

As I have shown through the few examples in this chapter, members of the law and order branch have the propensity to lie, bribe, hold grudges, assault, kill and do many other things that belie their code of conduct. The problem lies when we excuse, justify, or refuse to punish their actions because of their positions. Instead of being lenient when they run afoul of the law, they should be punished to the fullest extent possible for breaking their oath of service.

These are just a few of them. Time or space would not permit to examine the discrepancies in prosecution and punishment in Goldsboro, NC. Like the white lawyer who killed his brother in a drunken fight, but still practices law to this day. I'm sure if he was another race and didn't have the connections, he would have at least done some time in prison.

Some are excluded from prosecution and allowed to commit crimes with impunity, while others are charged, prosecuted, convicted and sentenced severely. I am reminded as a child and teen, I would ride down North William Street and see the parking lots full of young white teens, drinking, drugging, partying, racing and committing all sorts of crimes. They were hardly ever harassed and it seems like the cops sat and watched them.

That is the disparity. When an entire area can be full of people committing crimes and nothing happens to them. But another group can have three teens standing on the corner and they get searched every time an officer sees them. This proves a lack of equity. Not saying that police should not try to prohibit criminal activities and the judicial system should not seek to prosecute them. Just make sure that there is equal targeting throughout all races, classes, and communities.

This chapter was about my hometown of Goldsboro. However, this disparity happens all across the United States. Some places are worse than others. I've had the privilege of visiting and living in many areas. This same issue of systematic political, judicial and police injustice and inequality also exist in the great state of Virginia.

Chapter 14

The Commonwealth

In the early 2000's I left the gritty, grimy, hopeless streets of Goldsboro, and moved to Virginia Beach, VA. It was my goal to restart my life, leave my past behind and build a future in a new environment. The tourist location seemed ripe with opportunity, good vibes and new relationships.

I resided with my God brother, who stayed in an apartment complex near the city's up and coming town center. The neighborhood was nice and pleasant. I soon found a job at a Seven-eleven and another at a Norfolk shipyard. I quickly established a routine and found my place.

As I got comfortable, I realized that many of the same vices I left in Goldsboro were just as plentiful in Virginia Beach. I began to walk around the neighborhood and meet other teens and young adults who smoked weed, drank, and used other drugs like Ecstasy and coke. Before I knew it, I was in a similar circle of people that I ran with in my hometown.

Things really changed when I found a job at Ticketmaster, a huge call center in downtown Virginia Beach. This place was also filled with young high school or college students from all walks of life. It seemed like everyone in the building smoked marijuana and I quickly devised a plan to take advantage of it.

Through a connection I'd met at this job, I managed to buy a pound of weed. Next, I advertised to smokers at Ticketmaster and the neighborhood that I had product for sale. Word got around, one person introduced me to another, and before I knew it, I was a bona fide weed man, selling a pound or two a week.

During that time, one of my customers introduced me to a cocaine dealer, who wanted to buy weed. It was through this man, that I would begin using cocaine again. We developed a relationship and he took a liking to me.

Soon, I advertised to my customers that I had cocaine as well. Immediately, I had requests for the white powder. I began buying ounces from my new dealer friend. Seemingly overnight, less than a year of leaving Goldsboro, I had a steady flow of customers for coke and weed. I'd finally arrived, or so I thought.

The difference from my hometown and Virginia Beach was the Beach was a party town. As my business grew, it seemed everyone I met used drugs. From high school kids, to college students, businessmen, club owners, lawyers, funeral directors, detectives, strippers, and everyday laymen, users were plentiful. Most importantly, as it relates to the theme of the book, the majority of my customers were white, and from upscale families or positions in society.

Things went well, but inevitably, when you are doing wrong, problems occur. So let me reiterate that I in no way condone or excuse my actions. I lived the life I chose, and accept responsibility for my actions. I have suffered and some ways still suffer the consequences. These next situations are some of the issues I had to face, because of that lifestyle, but also because of the state of affairs in this country.

My first encounter with Virginia Beach police was due to a customer. They had come to buy weed. In the midst of the transaction, we had started a conversation and I had forgotten to get the money for the drugs.

When I called them back, they first denied it. When pressed, they finally admitted. Since they only stayed a few blocks away, I walked over to retrieve the money. I reached the apartment of the two white lesbians, and their friend, ironically named Ricky, in just a few minutes.

I was angry because I felt like they tried to play me. When the young white male opened the door, I entered without being asked. I got the money and gave them a piece of my mind. The man, Ricky, said something smart that I considered disrespectful. In my anger, I grabbed him by the shirt and started beating him.

The affray didn't last long as he didn't put up a fight. I left and headed home. In the back of my mind I knew I made a mistake. My fear came true after I was home for about thirty minutes.

There was a knock on my door. One look through the peephole confirmed that it was the police. I grabbed the only bag of marijuana I had in the house and proceeded to the back door of the apartment. As soon as I exited, a policeman was waiting. I attempted to run but there was no use. I surrendered, was searched and taken to the police precinct.

The police took me to an interrogation room, where a detective appeared. Apparently, the trio had told them all about my operation in addition to the fight. The first thing the police did was tell me that they knew I sold drugs. Then, they encouraged me to give up my connections. I refused and was charged with simple possession and released.

This is an example of how the police can use criminals to pursue charges on others, while excusing the activities of the former. Clearly, if the white friends knew I was selling drugs, they were using and buying. But the police were willing to overlook their crimes and focus on me. As well, they were willing to let me go, to get my supplier. If the objective is law and order, then everyone involved in crimes should be prosecuted.

The next encounter with police in Virginia Beach was somewhat similar. I had sold some cocaine to a young white man, who had got caught with the drug. Under the same pressure that I endured, he submitted and agreed to set me up. A week later, I got a call from the guy, eerily named Rick again. He told me he wanted a half ounce of coke. Though it was an unusually large order, my greed blinded me to the clear warning signs.

After he called, I got another call from another young white guy who wanted weed. Because I didn't have license at the time, I instructed him to come and get the weed but also take me to a nearby hotel to meet Rick for the coke sale. He agreed, but in hindsight considering how things transpired, he might have been in cahoots with the first caller.

The weed buyer arrived and we headed to the motel. I called Rick and he directed me around the side of the Days Inn to a certain room number. As soon as we rounded the corner, the vehicle was swarmed by a brown minivan and a few police cars.

Thinking fast, I stuffed the gram sized bag of cocaine I was sniffing into the cushion of the back seat. The half-ounce of coke was swiftly transferred from my lap into the confines of my boxer briefs. By the time the police pulled everyone out of the car, all cocaine was out of sight.

We were all taken into a hotel room. There was no Rick in sight. We were each individually taken into the bathroom, questioned and searched. I was the last one and waited on the couch. When it was my turn, I was sure that I would be stripped searched and the cocaine would be found.

To my surprise, the search was a lackluster. In the bathroom, the officer merely searched my pockets, socks and shoes and ran his fingers around the waistline of my underwear. I gave an inward sigh of relief as I was led out of the bathroom and released from the premises.

I later found that no one was charged with the cocaine left in the car. That gave me further reason to believe that I was the target and the other occupants of the car were complicit with the sting. Still, a few days later, I would see one of the men I was with and he would brag about nobody going to jail. Once again, the problems of some being free to do what they want, and others being targeted for the same activities were at play.

These and other incidents caused me to look for another residence. I found a one bedroom apartment only five blocks from the Virginia Beach oceanfront. It was here that my business grew exponentially, as I joined the party scene and began to rub shoulders with some of the illegal and legal power brokers of the city. I soon came to find out that those lines were often blurred and obscure.

For an example, I was once brought to the home of a prospective buyer by a regular customer of mine. When we entered the man's garage, I noticed a motorcycle with the license tag that read "1 Good Cop." My friend noticed the look on my face and offered reassurance.

"Don't worry, Rick. He's cool."

Reluctantly, I sold and used drugs with the off-duty police officer. Just like in Goldsboro, I was having a firsthand experience with the criminality of someone who was supposed to uphold the law.

Before I'd find out how deep things were, I'd go through the regular everyday harassment by police. Once I was riding in a car with my five friends, all of us black, down a main city road in Virginia Beach. We were pulled over by the police for no reason.

Even though the driver was licensed, all five of us were pulled from the car and searched. While we sat on the curb, the driver informed us that his legally registered handgun was in a book bag on the floor. When the officer's found it, they checked it, dismantled it and gave it back before letting us go. They never gave a reason for the stop or search, and we didn't ask, just happy to be out of the situation.

A similar situation didn't end well for me. After moving down by the beach, I bought a

Lincoln Town Car. Even though I didn't have license I was still able to get the car titled and registered in my name. I drove the car sparingly, only when necessary.

One day, after an evening of partying with a female acquaintance, I agreed to take her home. The only issue was that she lived in Newport News, about four cities away. Disregarding the potential peril, I embarked on the 45 minute ride over the Hampton Bridge and through the tunnel.

As soon as I reached the city of Newport News I got pulled over by the police. The reason the white man gave for the stop was that my license plate was crooked. That was it. The minute flaw was all that the officer needed to justify the stop. I suppose the black man, driving the big shiny car with the pretty white female passenger had nothing to do with it.

Nevertheless, I didn't argue. I provided the registration and the insurance and informed that I didn't have a license. He ran my name and found a warrant for a failure to appear on a domestic violence charge from Virginia Beach. I had gotten in a dispute with a former girlfriend a year earlier and neglected to go to court. The officer took me to jail for driving without license and the warrant.

I was given a 10,000 dollar bond for the driving charge. I got a trusted white customer to go to my house, get some money and post the $1000 needed for bail. I was then held in the Newport News jail until Virginia Beach came to extradite me for the warrant. They had fifteen days to get me and they came on the fourteenth. I was then given the same $10,000 bond for that charge after waiting two weeks for a bond hearing. I posted the bail and was released. The domestic violence case was eventually dismissed and I paid a fine for the driving charge.

After many dangerous instances and brushes with the law, I realized I needed to change my life again. Many of my associates were going to jail, robbing and even killing each other. I was even the victim of break-ins and robbery attempts by people I knew.

In 2005, I decided to take a real estate course to become a broker. I passed the four month class with flying colors as well as the subsequent state board test. I applied for licensure, which was denied because of the felony from seven years earlier. As stated before, the label of felon follows you for life and can handicap a person who is trying to change their life. This was one of those cases.

I made an appeal to the board and had a hearing. I brought letters of recommendation from very prominent and respectable references. My license was again refused in lieu of another meeting with the board. After that second appearance, I received a letter a few weeks later that I was given licensure. I was elated and began my life as an agent.

That was July, 2005. However, earlier that year, I had attempted to buy a handgun from a pawn shop. I gave the money, filled out the paperwork and waited the twenty minutes for results from the SBI on a record check. I knew I had the felony in North Carolina, but was unclear if that would deny me a gun permit in Virginia. It did.

The manager returned my money and I left the store. I thought nothing more of it. The issue resurfaced a few months after I received my real estate license and a few weeks after I listed my first house for sale.

In November, I attended a trip to Indianapolis with some close friends and family. My childhood friend played for the Colts and we were invited to the Sunday morning game. However, the night before, I and his brother went to grab a bite to eat. I had never been to White Castle so I chose the famed burger joint.

When we arrived, we noticed a car full of young white men in the parking lot. They were drinking and being loud and disruptive. We ignored the men, went in the restaurant and ordered, and then stepped back outside into the Indiana night. By that time, the car full of partiers had left.

Less than five minutes later, two Indiana State troopers drove into the parking lot and pulled directly up to me and my friend. The two stout white men got out of the car and walked towards us. I thought, "Oh Lord," in my mind as one began to speak.

"Howdy!! We had a report of someone causing a disturbance in the parking lot. Do y'all know anything about that," one said with a redneck accent.

"No we don't," I answered. "There was a car over there being loud, but it wasn't us."

"So what are y'all doing out here?"

"We just came to get something to eat. We're up here for the game tomorrow, to see the Colts. I came from Virginia and he's from North Carolina. We're not looking for any trouble," I said.

At this point in my life, I had given up all criminal activity. I was a regular citizen who wanted to prove that he could be an asset and not a threat to society. This led me to hand the officers my identification voluntarily, while my friend did the same. They took the cards and went back to their vehicle.

"Mr. Taylor, put your hands behind your back," one said as the two returned.

Instead of me, they grabbed my friend who looked astonished. I guess it's true what they say. According to white people and police, all blacks look alike. I quickly intervened.

"No, I am Richard Taylor. What's the matter?

"Did you ever try to buy a gun in Virginia Beach?"

"Yes, but they didn't let me get it. That's not a crime is it," I inquired.

The officer informed me that there was a warrant out for my arrest in Virginia for "attempting to possess a firearm by a felon." He said that I was going to be detained until it was verified. If they didn't send confirmation, I would be let go.

Unfortunately the warrant confirmed. I was led away in handcuffs and transported to the county jail of Indianapolis. Understandably upset, I gave the officers a hard time on the ride. In turn, they stripped me of the $500 Movado watch I had purchased months earlier. I missed the game, and never got my property back.

I waited for two weeks to be extradited to Virginia. They had the same fifteen days to come get me and arrived on the fourteenth day. The officers from Virginia, one black and one white received the same treatment. I belittled their choice of profession, the futility of their visit, and their purpose in life. It got so bad, the white man turned to me with a threat of his own.

"Look, our only job is to bring your body back to Virginia. It doesn't matter how we do it, as long as your body comes back with us, our job is done."

The emphasis that he placed on the word body made his threat clear and present. He had the ability and the authority to kill me. I was nothing but a common criminal and prisoner in his and the law's sight. The black official glanced back and gave me a look that said just be quiet. He completely ignored the unlawful, unprofessional actions of his partner.

I was transported by plane back to Virginia and placed in the Virginia Beach jail again. I was given a $5000 bond for the class F felony, which is only one step above a misdemeanor. I was freed on bail. Months later, I pled no contest to the charge and received a fine and 12 months unsupervised probation.

I interjected this encounter for a couple of reasons. One is to highlight the automatic assumption of the Indiana troopers that the black men outside of the restaurant were the subjects of the disturbance. This was definitely a result of the training, stereotypical beliefs and the propaganda that the men received and accepted.

The second reason is the charge that I received and the willingness to prosecute me for the least of offenses. I hurt no one in attempting to buy a gun legally. I could have easily bought one off the streets. However the state was willing to spend money on transporting me from a thousand miles away to secure a conviction. The threat from the white officer upon my life needs no examination.

After this incident I continued my quest at restoration. I stayed trouble free for the next three years. In 2008, I met my child's mother. A few months later we were expecting my daughter. In the interim, I lost my job. With no other immediate way to make the kind of money I was making, I returned to dealing.

At this point, I won't get into the particular details of my choice. It has already been established that the criminal lifestyle is detrimental and destructive to the participant and the surrounding community. Nevertheless, six months into my run, On October 31, 2008 my life was changed forever. I was shot three times at close range while holding my three month old daughter during a robbery.

The details of this and other dangerous situations I faced are outlined in my first novel "Brushes with Death: The Blood of Jesus." As a result of the shooting, I was charged with a half-ounce of cocaine that was found in my underwear when the paramedics tended to me. The technician seemed more concerned with the golf-ball sized amount of drugs than with the liters of blood spilling from my body.

The assailant was arrested a few blocks away from the scene of the crime, with the bloody money in her possession. I was taken to the hospital and miraculously released a few days later without serious injury. Less than a week later, police came and charged me with the possession with intent to sell and distribute cocaine.

I posted another $10,000 bond and immediately moved back to Goldsboro. I wanted to change my life and reflect how I had gotten to that situation. That's when I started writing my first novel.

I can't remember whose trial came first, mines or my attacker's. The disposition of the cases in Virginia Beach court highlights the disparity and the inequity in the judicial system. The woman who had shot me three times, put an infant's life in danger and robbed me with a dangerous weapon, pled no contest and only received an eight-year prison sentence.

Meanwhile my charges were dropped from intent to distribute to simple possession. It wasn't bagged for resale, so the charge was never supposed to be levied in that manner. My lawyer presented a plea agreement for an eight-year suspended sentence with eight-years of supervised probation. Not wanting to risk jail time, I accepted the agreement, knowing the ramifications. The terms meant that I could not get into any trouble for an eight year period or I risked being sentenced to the full term.

Things went well for a while. My probation was transferred to North Carolina. I made the appointments, kept a job and paid the fines. After being denied a North Carolina real estate license due to my record, I grew discouraged and went through the situations I mentioned in the last chapter. Two and a half years passed and I decided to move back to Virginia.

Once more, I'm the first to admit that I went back with ill intentions. It was the 4th of July and I had an ounce of cocaine to sell. I called a few of my old customers, who were more than happy to hear from me. I set up the orders and jumped back into the swing of things like I never left.

After meeting all of my customers, I got up with the crew I used to run with. We went to the beach and later went to an after hour strip party. I still had about a gram to use for my own personal purposes. I enjoyed the festivities, but as we were leaving a shootout erupted between two enemies.

During the melee, I ran and got separated from the people I rode with. I found myself running down Virginia Beach Blvd away from the scene. I called my people that I had come with, but they were already on the way to the hospital. One of my comrades was shot.

I continued to walk down the street until a police cruiser rolled up on me. He immediately got out and asked the usual questions; where was I going, where was I coming from? I gave him a random answer along with my identification. Thinking I was in the clear, I waited the return of my card so I could leave.

The officer informed me that I had a warrant for a probation violation. This stemmed from the incident in Goldsboro where I was charged with driving without license after being pulled over and brushing the side of my friend's house. I had pled guilty to it, thinking that a simple driving charge in North Carolina wouldn't be enough to violate the probation in Virginia. I was wrong.

Once again, I found myself heading to the Virginia Beach jail for something I had done. However, I could argue that the police had no business stopping me in the first place. If they are responding to a shots fired call, why does the black man walking down the street have to be the immediate suspect?

I reached the jail and went through the booking process as I had many times before. The magistrate issued a $5000 bond. When I got downstairs I called my bondsman, who told me he would be there in the morning. It was already about 4 am, so I only had a few hours to wait. I was placed in a holding cell, awaiting bail, or placement on a floor, whichever came first.

I then realized that I had the bag of cocaine stuffed by my genitals in my boxer briefs. I should have flushed it down the toilet, but one doesn't always make the best decisions when high on drugs. I figured I could keep it for use upon my release.

However, an hour later, a guard came to the cell and told me that I was going to be dressed out. I was led to the property room and instructed to take off my clothes to be searched. Now, I faced a dilemma with the illegal substance in my possession. I had to think fast.

I took off my socks and shoes and handed them to the deputy. He inspected them, while I removed my shirt and tank top. He turned them inside out and shook them, as I removed my pants. When I handed them to him, I removed my boxers real fast, cuffing the drugs in my right hand. I intended to transfer the bag to my mouth and swallow it while he wasn't looking.

I wasn't fast enough. The guard noticed my moves and before I got my hand to my mouth, he jumped on me and started yelling for help. I still managed to get the bag into my mouth before five or six more deputies entered the room.

I still tried to swallow, but due to the drug usage and the dryness of my mouth, I couldn't muster enough saliva to get it down. One deputy jumped on my back and pulled my chin up in a Boston Crab wrestling move position. Another grabbed my arms and pinned them behind my back. Yet another wrapped his hands around my throat to prevent me from swallowing and another pried at my lips with his hands.

By this time, I started chewing the bag. The potent substance penetrated my gums, numbing my entire mouth. I still fought literally tooth and nail to keep my mouth shut. The nurse rushed in with a tongue depressor and tried to force it between my pursed lips.

Then, something happened to let me know how evil these people were. The officer on my back took one hand and pinched the nostrils of my nose together so I couldn't breathe. I twisted and turned my head trying to loosen his grip. Before I passed out from lack or air, I opened my mouth with a huge gasp. The nurse then placed the depressor down my throat, literally choking me in an attempt to get the drugs.

By then, all that remained was the plastic bag with white, slimy residue inside. I was taken to the medical ward due to the cocaine in my system. They threw me in a dungeon like cell, completely naked, with a mat and a green tarp like suit. They also held me down and injected me with something that they would not let me turn around and view. I still wonder today what that substance was.

Nevertheless I stayed in that cell for three days, until I was deemed ready for the population by the medical staff. I was soon brought back before the magistrate on a charge of possession of cocaine by an inmate. I stayed in jail for nearly six months before being released on time served.

I learned much from this experience. The main lesson was that the deputies in jail were willing to kill in order to secure a conviction. If I had died while the deputies choked and denied me air, the story would have been that I choked on the cocaine I tried to swallow. They would have conveniently left out their part in the matter. My question is, was getting the cocaine so important to the officers that they were willing to kill me in order to do it.

Two months into my confinement, another inmate was found dead in her cell. The news reports stated that she choked on the state issued wristband given to inmates for identification. Just the sheer description of the situation seemed implausible. How does one choke on something that is secured on one's wrist? Considering what I had endured upon my entrance, I could only imagine what really happened.

Also, I realized that the county jail had been turned into a detention center. That meant they could hold inmates for up to five years upon sentencing. The reason for this was to get more money from the state, but also to get income from canteen orders, phone calls and other amenities the jail provided for prisoners. They're were men with four year sentences and served all their time in the Virginia Beach jail.

I also had to suffer through the everyday inhumane treatment from guards and the like. The court appointed lawyers that were assigned were equally inept and once again only offered pleas. My stay once again made me reevaluate my decisions and vow to live a more productive life.

Upon my release I had to report to a Virginia probation office. I informed them that I had nowhere to stay and I wanted to return to Goldsboro. The lady informed me that I couldn't leave the state and had to find somewhere in the city of Norfolk to live. With no alternative, I returned to live with my daughter and her mother until I could get on my feet.

For the next year and a half, I worked hard. I stayed clean, enrolled in school and finished the book I started in 2009. In November of 2012, I had my first book signing. In February of 2013 I performed my first paid speaking engagement at the school I was attending, Tidewater Community College. I promoted my work and got a lot of support from everyone. Things were looking up, until June 1st of the same year.

That is the day that I was charged with a crime that I didn't commit. After a domestic dispute, a female acquaintance accused me of rape, kidnapping, abduction, abduction with intent to defile, assault, and other misdemeanors. I was taken to jail without any evidence and held without bond on the basis of her word. My life had once again come to a screeching legal halt.

The details of the entire story are relayed in my second novel "Wrongfully Accused, Rightfully Acquitted." Therefore I won't go to in depth about the situation. However, I will point out a couple of main points to highlight the injustices I faced.

The first problem was the court appointed lawyer. On his first visit via video conference he never looked me in the eye, and never asked me what happened. He just asked me some vague questions. When I attempted to explain the situation, he informed me he had to go, and hung up the virtual call.

Two months went by before I heard from him again. This time it was the day before the preliminary hearing to determine if there was enough evidence to go to trial. He again never looked me in the eye. He did offer a proposition that was typical of every court appointed lawyer that I'd had.

"Well, they've offered you a deal, and I think it's a pretty good one. If you waive the preliminary hearing and plead guilty tomorrow, they've offered you a sentence of nine to twenty-seven years. I think you should take it."

"Mr. Hallock," I responded in shock. "I didn't do this. You never even asked me what happened. Do you even remember me? Last time you hung up the phone on me!"

"Well, I have to go now too. See you tomorrow in court."

With his last statement the screen went blank. I couldn't believe it. Here I was facing the rest of my life in prison, and my only advocate had hung up the phone on me twice. It was at that point that I decided to defend myself in the preliminary hearing the next day.

I did so despite the objection of the prosecutor. I performed well and asked the witness questions that would prove perjury when the evidence surfaced. However, afterwards, I received no assistance from the court appointed lawyer in securing essential proof of my innocence.

Two months had passed. I'd asked for the motion of discovery, which is all the evidence that the state had against me. I'd asked for the phone records between me and the alleged victim. I also requested the DNA results. The lawyer's response was that he could not obtain them. Most of my calls went unanswered by him and I only spoke with the secretary.

A month before the trial was to start I was awakened to attend court. When I arrived, the lawyer came to see me and informed that he was asking for a continuance until January of the next year. I told him I didn't want a continuance and preferred my right to a speedy trial.

See, I did the research. If you're being held without bond, the state is obligated to bring you to trial within 150 days or they have to let you free. The only way that right is void is if the defense asks for a continuance. This is a tactic used by defense lawyers to deny the rights of their clients and give the state time to build a case. Like in the case of my cousin, I have seen guys stay in jail for years awaiting trial for this reason. I would not be one of them.

Upon entering the court I informed the judge that I did not want a continuance and I also wanted to fire the lawyer. The judge agreed and assigned me to Thomas Reid, a renowned lawyer, who just happened to be on the pro bono list that day. As I was being led away, I saw my ex lawyer turn to the prosecutor and apologize.

"He wouldn't let me do it," he said in defeat. Then and there his actions made sense. It was already agreed that he would push for a plea, or provide a lackluster defense, and I would be sent away for life for a crime I didn't commit.

The next day the new lawyer came to see me. He bypassed the video monitors and took the elevator to the 7th floor of Norfolk's jail to meet with me face to face. We talked for an hour. He actually listened to me as I did to him. We got to know each other personally. I told him what I needed and he vowed to get the information.

Less than a week later, I had everything I asked of the previous lawyer. He had the motion of discovery, the phone records, and the DNA results. I talked to him weekly on the phone and we discussed the strategic ways that we could prove my innocence. I felt a confidence that I hadn't felt since the day of the arrest

I will skip the experiences of the jail, the unsanitary conditions, inhumane treatment by the guards, and other nuances of inmate life. That can be revisited in the aforementioned book. The first day of the trial is what we'll examine next.

While I sat in the holding cell, before the jury was selected, the guards let my lawyer in. He brought news that was both encouraging and disturbing. I listened as he came to the gate.

"Good morning, Richard. I just wanted to tell you, that the prosecutor has offered a deal. It's a pretty good one too. She's agreed to drop the rape, kidnapping, abduction, and the abduction with intent to defile. All you have to do is plead guilty to a simple assault and you'll walk out of here today."

I listened to the proposition. It sounded like a good deal. Rather than risk a life sentence in a trial, I could plead guilty to something I didn't do, and walk out of the jail immediately. The only problem was that a guilty plea would violate my probation, and I wouldn't be released anyway. I explained this to him, and asked a question of my own.

"Why is she agreeing to drop all the charges and let me go free?"

"Because," Mr. Reed answered. "She knows its bullshit."

So there you have it. Even though the prosecutor knew I was innocent, her job was not to seek justice, but to get a conviction. We proceeded through the trial. I watched the same woman that was about to let me go free paint me as a monster who deserved lifetime imprisonment to the jury.

Fortunately they didn't believe her. After a week-long trial, I was found not guilty on all charges. I cried as the verdict was read, while the accuser who perjured herself many times on the stand walked out of the courtroom unscathed. I felt no ill will. I was just elated to have escaped with my life; having not been railroaded by an unjust prosecutor and a complicit court appointed lawyer.

After this, I attempted to move back to North Carolina again. I was denied for the second time. My probation sentence of eight years had restarted upon my conviction in 2011. So instead of three more years of probation, I had six.

That's the other problem with Virginia's laws. They keep you in the system with probation.

Under their statutes, if a person had 20 years of probation, and messes up on the 19th year, he would have to start the 20-year period over again, in essence giving him forty years of supervision. This is egregious and should not be allowed. Nevertheless, I stayed still under the threat of the law.

I soon secured a job with a timeshare company. I quickly moved up the ranks and started making decent money. I got my license back, reenrolled in school and graduated with an Associate's degree in 2015. I even bought a car in the summer of that year.

It wasn't just any car though. It was a souped-up black Impala with suicide doors, 24 inch rims, crocodile seats, and Chrome everywhere. I always wanted something flashy like that, but didn't want to draw attention to myself. Now, I figured since I didn't sell drugs anymore, it wouldn't be a problem. Wrong again!

I got stopped a total of five times in a six month period of having the car. I won't go into every situation, but I will expound on the most blatant case of racial profiling and the officer's justification.

It was Halloween night and I was leaving the Oceanfront. Before getting on the interstate, I passed a police officer. We looked each other in the face. I learned over the years, that action was a definite no-no; never look an officer in his eyes. You are either intimidating or suspicious and he's coming for you.

He immediately turned around and got behind me. Within seconds, he hit the blue lights. I quickly pulled over, having my license, insurance and registration at the ready. I handed him the items as he gave me the bogus reason for the stop.

"The reason I pulled you over is because one of your license plate lights are out."

I just shook my head and waited for him to come back from his car. Since I was legit, I didn't even mind the ticket. I didn't even bother to ask the obvious question. I just thought it to myself.

Why did you even turn around to get behind me in the first place? There was no way he could see that little light was out from the front of the car. And, he turned around before I even passed him all the way. The miniscule flaw was just a reason to justify his unlawful and evil racial profiling of the black man with the shiny car and the big rims.

I eventually sold the car because of all the harassment. I purchased a Volkswagon Jetta and had fewer problems on the road. However, I would soon have issues with the probation system.

One day I was told that my officers would be switched. Instead of the white women, who only ask one or two questions on the five minute visits, I was switched to a black man who proved to be much more menacing. On the first visit, he greeted me with a cup as soon as I walked through the door.

"What is this," I asked surprisingly.

"This is for a urine screen. Sign your initials on the label and go into the first door on the right. I'll come to the window with the cup."

Out of the six years of probation, I had never been drug tested. Though I wasn't selling anymore, I still used cocaine and weed occasionally. It had gotten worse as I worked at the oceanfront hotels, where everybody partied: tourists, co-workers, bosses, and locals. This was the beginning of a long four years with Mr. Johnson.

He was lenient though. He could have violated me for that first positive. Instead, he talked to me and gave me incentives. But I had a drug problem. Even though I knew when I would be tested, I still couldn't stop using. He enrolled me in counseling and threatened violation constantly, but I was sick.

I insert this here to show the hypocrisy. Drug use is a disease. Yet, another probationer may have sent me to jail for the first failure. Even though I was working, not getting in trouble, paying taxes and not harming anyone but myself, I could be jailed. This is the reason for the outrage over the thousands of non-violent drug offenders in jail or prison today.

Eventually, after eleven negatives, and three counseling groups, he sent the paperwork to Virginia Beach in the summer of 2019. I was due to get off in November of that year. Unfortunately, the Virginia Beach office violated my probation three months before my release.

How I found out, was even more startling. I had moved to Norfolk earlier that year, into a neighborhood that wasn't so nice. As I was coming home from work, I passed a police officer a block from my house. I made the dreaded mistake of looking at him. He drove a block down then busted a U-turn.

I knew he was coming for me. I pulled quickly in front of my building and exited the car. I went into my apartment and watched as the police drove slowly by. When I felt he'd left, I went back to my car to get my charger. I noticed the officer down the street watching. I got my things and walked back to my door while the officer sped toward me.

I went into the house and a few seconds later, I heard the loud boom of the policeman knocking on the door. I answered immediately not knowing about the warrant. He asked me was I the driver of the car. When I told him yes, he cuffed me and told me about the warrant for probation violation.

While he waited for confirmation, we chatted. I asked him, why he turned around when he saw me initially? He gave a vague answer. Then I asked him why did he run my tags? He replied that he always did that when he got behind someone. I didn't even address it because I knew the truth and had endured it for many years. The white officer was patrolling the black neighborhood, looking for the first opportunity to pull a black man over to find him doing something wrong.

Long story short, I was jailed without bond for two months, awaiting trial. My court appointed lawyer told me that I was at least facing one and half to two years. In addition to that, my probation sentence would start over again and I'd have eight more years.

However, when we got to court, the judge looked at the case and wondered why my sentence would be so high. I had no new charges and had only failed drug tests. It was uncovered that I was given sentence increases for the rape, kidnapping and abduction charges I was acquitted of. Even though I was found not guilty, the prosecutor explained that was part of the guidelines.

"Why is he being punished for something that he did not do," the judge questioned. "Isn't that unconstitutional?"

The prosecutor shrugged his shoulders. The judge let me know verbally, that if he had the power to sentence me, he definitely wouldn't give me two years. He then reiterated that he wouldn't give me a year. It was then that I decided to reject the plea agreement and leave my sentencing in the judge's hands.

The just official didn't give me any jail time. He let me out on condition of two years good behavior. The most important thing that he did was release me from probation altogether. He said that I had not been a detriment to society, but I just needed help with a drug problem. He wished me success in my future and adjourned the case. I went on to attend a recovery program voluntarily, and here I am today.

The judge's decision in my last and final case was the example of true justice. Even though the statutes and laws mandated one outcome, he took the authority and examined my case individually. He looked at me as a person and not based on the statistics, numbers, or my record. Many judges have the power to do the same thing in most cases, but they often lean toward harshness rather than leniency.

The previous two chapters have been laced with interactions between me, police and the legal system. I included my transgressions willfully and transparently to show culpability in many of those encounters. However, after my actions, there still has to be a certain level or respect, honor, equity and fairness of those who hold public office or are trained professionals.

Other instances in this chapter display the wanton and malicious behavior of police, lawyers, prosecutors, judges and the like. Whether being stopped for no reason, falsely arrested in the courthouse for speaking one's mind, being beaten or shocked by officers while in custody, neglected or wrongfully persuaded by court appointed lawyers, unfairly or excessively prosecuted by state attorneys, overly sentenced by judges, punished for things you didn't do, paying three and four times for one crime, outright killed by police and the many other offenses of state officials highlighted in these chapters, there has to be an acknowledgement that these things do occur and a concerted effort to bring them to an end.

These are just a few of the injustices I've seen and experienced in my life. There is no way I could list all the unlawful things that have occurred to me at the hands of the judicial system, no more than I could list all of the crimes that I've committed over the years. In this regard, I am thankful for the 25 years that I've spent engrossed and battling the legal system. In that time I have been privy to expose things that some will never know about, more less believe.

If all of these situations happened to one man, just imagine the countless others who have had similar experiences. Some are not able to articulate their stories. Some do not have the platform. Some have been silenced by years in prison or even the grave. Others may have just given up and accepted the status quo. Most of their plights have been swept away under the rugs of their local city or state governments.

However, there is a new dawn that has arisen in the last several years. With the advent of the cell phone camera, social media and alternative media outlets, America is getting an unbridled look at the dirty underbelly of the law enforcement system firsthand. The brutality and cruelty of police tactics are displayed live and in color in the homes of those who could have never fathomed.

The evil is too blatant to ignore. The outcry is too loud to not hear. The fire is too hot not to burn the skin of everyone in its reach. The average everyday American is witnessing the horrors that many have lived with for years.

In contrast to the judge who showed mercy and leniency to me in my last case, the officials in the recent high profiled cases have shown no restraint. They have used their position and the legal system that backs them, to be the judge, jury, and executioner of those who crossed their paths. The next chapters are dedicated to those who lost their lives at the hands of those who are supposed to protect.

Chapter 15

Trayvon, Omar, Mike, Eric

I was born on February 26, 1978. On my 34th birthday, events transpired that shook the nation and exposed the experiences of black males in America like no one had ever seen. On this day in 2012, a part time security guard who wanted to be a cop, tracked, hunted and killed a 17-year old boy named Trayvon Martin.

Details were sketchy at first. As evidence emerged, the public gained more knowledge of the happenings on that dark night. It all started with a trip through the neighborhood, by a young man who only wanted skittles and a drink from a nearby store.

During his return to his father's house, he was followed by the neighborhood watchman and soon to be killer, George Zimmerman. George apparently called 911 and informed them of the suspicious teen with the now trademarked hoodie. In the released taped call, the dispatcher clearly told him not to follow the child. Zimmerman completely ignored the official and continued in pursuit.

George's pursuit led to an encounter between the two. There was a confrontation; a physical altercation. Some reports and theories say that the teen was getting the best of the older man. However, audio from the incident emitted screaming from what seemed like a child-like voice. No matter who made the noise the night ended with the teenage Martin dead with a gunshot through the heart.

Zimmerman was picked up that night but released without being charged. After weeks of public outrage, he was arrested and charged with second degree murder. He was given a $150,000 bond which was later revoked and reinstated at a million. He stayed in jail until the trial date which was in May of 2013.

During the interim a wave of information surfaced and the propaganda began. Photos surfaced of Zimmerman the night of the murder with a bloodied head. He stated that the injuries came from the teen slamming his head repeatedly against the concrete. He told investigators, he felt that he was going to die.

To compliment George's assertion of being the victim, the media began a smear campaign of Trayvon's character. They reportedly found pictures in his phone of marijuana and a gun. They constantly flashed menacing pictures of the child in a hoodie. They even inferred that the pack of skittles and the Arizona drink in his possession were the ingredients for some concoction called lean, an intoxicating mixture including promethazine.

So the stage was set. The predator that followed an unsuspecting kid on his way home, initiated a confrontation, and shot the child in cold blood was painted as the helpless concerned citizen that feared for his life in the presence of the big, black, super strong, drug addicted Trayvon. Hence, the infamous "stand your ground," defense was initiated by his team.

Florida's "stand your ground" law is a statute that allows a person to use deadly force if they feel their life is in danger. Zimmerman's claim that he feared for his life after instigating a conflict is altogether ludicrous. However, 15 months after the killing, the law would set the perpetrator free.

The trial was held in the city of Sanford in Seminole County, Florida. The city has a population of twice as many whites as blacks. On July 20, 2013, a jury of six white women, and four alternates were selected to hear the case. It seemed like the deck was stacked from the beginning.

I won't dissect the particulars of the trial. The proceedings lasted for fifteen days. The jury was released and after only sixteen hours of deliberation, returned with a not guilty verdict. The decision sparked outrage and dismay throughout black communities nationwide.

The stand your ground law became the subject of much debate. It seemed the law only worked for white defendants. In May of 2012, just a year before the Zimmerman verdict, a Florida woman, who was black, was sentenced to a mandatory 20 years in prison for aggravated assault after the stand your ground defense was rejected. Her crime; she fired a warning shot into the air after her estranged husband broke into her home, attacked and threatened to kill her.

How can one person chase another down and the defense be accepted, but another defends her own home without hurting the attacker and be denied. Zimmerman was found to have done nothing unlawful in the murder of Trayvon Martin. Apparently, killing a black man that you initiated conflict with was perfectly within George's rights. The Dred Scott decision was in full effect here; a black man had no rights that are to be respected. Consequently this verdict would set the precedent for many cases in the future and beyond.

Right around the time that Zimmerman was set free, a lesser publicized incident occurred that devastated the Norfolk, VA Park Place community I was then a part of. On May 20, 2013, 22 year-old Joshua "Omar" Johnson was shot and killed by Norfolk Police officer Matthew Watson. In what has become a popular ruling, the officer's actions were ruled justified in the shooting death of an unarmed black male.

According to police and media reports, Johnson and his girlfriend were in the drive through

lane at a Wells Fargo bank in the prestigious
neighborhood of Ghent. Allegedly, the two
attempted to pass a forged check in the amount of
two-hundred dollars. The teller noticed the
attempted fraud, held the check and notified the
police, unbeknownst to the couple.

Law enforcement arrived within minutes
and surrounded the car with guns drawn. In an
attempt to retreat, Johnson put the car in reverse and
started to back away. In the process, he reportedly
hit an officer. In response, the officer's partner fired
a total of eleven rounds into the vehicle, hitting
Johnson in the head, chest, neck and other parts of
the body.

Joshua was pronounced dead at the scene.
His girlfriend miraculously survived the barrage
unscathed. Word quickly spread to the surrounding
community of Park Place, where people who knew
the deceased wanted answers. Why was a good
young man from all accounts dead over a worthless
check? Why did police come to the scene with guns
drawn in the first place?

I had a hands-on experience with the case.
Joshua lived only a few blocks from my apartment.
His family stayed on 27th street, I lived on 34th. He
cut hair at the same barbershop I patronized. I didn't
know him personally, but I knew a lot of his family,
close personal friends and associates. The people

who loved him began to organize rallies, marches, and memorial events in his name.

I was privy to the action because I lived so close. I was a student at the time, promoting my first book. I attended many of the functions in Omar's honor, at times speaking to audiences and news media in front of his residence. I even got an opportunity to speak with his mother, sister and girlfriend. I saw the pain and misery of the situation firsthand.

The lead catalyst in the call for "Justice for Omar," was a well-known community activist named Michael J. Muhammad. Having served the interests of the people for two and a half decades, Muhammad galvanized the community, addressed law enforcement, news media, and put pressure on city hall to charge the officer involved. Most importantly, he demanded that law enforcement release the surveillance tapes of the shooting.

Unfortunately, no officer was ever charged. Despite the outcry, the police department refused to release the video footage. However, they did engage in the same smear campaign as always; displaying mugshots of the girlfriend after the shooting, and bringing up minor infractions of the deceased in the past.

Eventually, due to Muhammad's persistence the video was released in February of 2014. No portion of the video was ever shown publicly, only to Johnson's lawyer. According to police, the video corroborated the officer's story. However, the girlfriend contradicted the account of police. She insisted that police pulled up with guns drawn and immediately started firing into the car. Other accounts say that Omar didn't hit an officer and barely had a chance to react before he was fired upon.

To this day, no justice has been served. A civil lawsuit was settled for $163,000. This also seems to be a tactic. These payments are a way of the state admitting guilt, while at the same time avoiding punishment and silencing the family. In this case, the police were able to act as judge, jury, and executioner of a man with no defender. Even though attempting to cash a bad check is wrong, it is not a capital offense.

About a year after Johnson's murder, the country would be stunned once more. In Ferguson, Missouri, on August 9, 2014, eighteen year-old Mike Brown was shot in cold blood by Officer Darren Wilson, a twenty-eight year old who already had numerous complaints. This shooting was magnified by media coverage of the dead body lying in the streets for nearly four hours, as officer's looked on.

Many conflicting accounts surfaced at the onset. One is the officer and Brown had an argument, in which Wilson shot him after the confrontation. Another says that Brown and Wilson got into a physical scuffle. Eventually Brown surrendered with his hands up, and in turn was shot. The officer claimed that he and Brown were in a fight in which Brown grabbed for his gun. Wilson says he feared for his life and shot Brown. No matter which story is true, Mike Brown died of six gunshot wounds, two of which were to the head.

Several eyewitnesses, black and white said that at the time of his death, the eighteen-year old had his hands up. However, many of these witnesses later recanted their testimony. Some like the friend who was with Brown, turned up missing or dead.

After the death, the media released video of a confrontation that the teenager had with a store owner. The footage showed Michael Brown snatching some cigars from behind the counter and attempting to leave the store. A small man tried to prevent him, but was easily pushed to the side by the larger Brown.

This video was used to paint the picture of Brown as a robbery suspect. However, later footage surfaced of Brown having an interaction with other workers at the store, trading some sort of product for the cigars. Apparently, there was a relationship between Brown and the workers that was unknown to the owner.

Nevertheless, the video was played day in and day out, cementing in the court of public opinion that Brown was a violent criminal that deserved to be killed in the street. The images also solidified the officer's perceived fear for his life from the big strong black boy. Despite testimonies, and evidence, the officer was never charged. Wilson was only fired and relocated to another location.

When news of the justification reached the streets, riots erupted all over the city of Ferguson, already rife with protestors. Many were arrested and others were killed. King Darren Seals, a major activist in Ferguson was found burned to death in his car. It was ruled a suicide and no one was charged in his death either. The Ferguson unrest was broadcast all over the nation, and sparked similar protests, nationwide.

Though no one was arrested in Brown's death, the act initiated a federal investigation into the Ferguson police department. Cases of police brutality, abuse of power, racial injustice, discrimination and inequalities in policing were exposed. The city vowed to make changes to include more black police officers in a department that was underrepresented by minorities.

Even though Mike Brown's murder was committed in the south, a police killing in the north just a month earlier would add fuel to the already burning fire in the United States. On Thursday, July

17th in Staten Island, NY, Eric Garner died at the hands of police after being choked to death on a live recorded video.

The 34 year old father was approached by NYPD on the streets. The reason for the interaction was that Garner was selling cigarettes or "looseys" on the corner. Since cigarettes were ten or twelve dollars a pack in New York, many people would sell cigarettes individually for a dollar a piece to make extra change or support their habits. It is a well-known hustle to many across the nation, and certainly not an offense worthy of death.

The video shows Garner being accosted by police, with him pleading for them to leave him alone. As he was walking away, he was grabbed from behind and wrestled to the ground. While being subdued by six officers, he was put in a chokehold. While he was not resisting, he begged and screamed to the officer, "I can't breathe." He repeated the phrase repeatedly until his cries went silent and life exited his body (ABC News).

The public was understandably outraged watching the video of six police officers on the back of one man. However, following normal protocol, they began to speak about Garner's previous legal issues. The media highlighted his 30 arrests and the fact that he was "selling untaxed cigarettes." The wording leads one to believe that it is a federal crime. However, it is a low-level misdemeanor. To add insult to injury, the department actually charged him posthumously for the minor offense.

After the investigation by the department of itself, and the smear campaign by the media, there was no charging of the officers. The chokehold was ruled justified and the officers involved remained on duty. Just like in Ferguson, the decision not to reprimand the officials sparked another round of protest and riots across the nation.

In these four cases, one of the main ingredients for the officers not being charged is the way the police and media, criminalized the victim. Whether it is fighting a guy who is following you, trying to pass a bad check, stealing cigars or selling cigarettes, none of those are capital offenses. However, painting these men as suspects, offenders, and focusing on their past indiscretions hardens the public perception of them and erases any sympathy for their death.

Also, the fact that prosecutors, grand juries, judges, police and investigators all work together in the same system, makes it nearly impossible for them to condemn themselves. Therefore, they do anything in their power to protect each other.

The hypocrisy of it all is the settlements that are paid out. Trayvon's family got an undisclosed amount of money. Mike Brown's parents received 1.5 million dollars. Lastly, Eric Garner's descendants got a whopping 5.9 million dollars. The fact that the state paid millions of dollars in "wrongful" death lawsuits is almost an admission of guilt. Contrarily, no white officer is ever charged for killing black men.

Three of these cases received national attention. Johnson's death, I would have probably never heard of had I not lived a few blocks away. I added his situation to show how the national example of not punishing rogue police officers trickles down to local municipalities, and gives them a blueprint of how to navigate these situations. As we shall see, towns and cities began to mimic the national examples and still do so to this day.

Chapter 16

Tamir, Walter, Freddy, Sandra

In the midst of the turmoil following the cases in the previous chapter, new episodes sprung up. None was more disturbing and senseless than the case of Tamir Rice. On November 22, 2014, the twelve year old boy was shot without reservation by a 26 year-old white police officer, Timothy Loehmann. His crime was playing alone in a park with a toy gun in broad daylight.

Like many killings before and after, the shooting was caught on tape. The footage shows a little boy alone in the park, walking innocently. Like a stealth bomber, a police officer pulled into view. Before exiting the vehicle fully, the officer fired a fatal shot, killing the young black male. No conversation, no dialogue; just a perceived threat by an overzealous trigger happy officer.

How did it all happen? A citizen called the Cleveland, OH police department and told the dispatcher that there was a boy in the park pointing a gun at people. The caller even specified that the gun looked like a fake. Nevertheless, this unknown caller is reminiscent of the current "Karen" phenomenon, where white women randomly call the police on black people who are doing nothing but minding their own business. If it were not for this call, Tamir would undoubtedly be alive today.

Unfortunately he is not. Despite the heinous footage and lack of threat, officer Loehmann was excused from any wrongdoing. Although he was subsequently fired, he was hired later by another Ohio Police Department in Bellaire. The only so-called justice received by the Rice family was a 6 million dollar settlement from the city of Cleveland.

Rice's death added a fuse to the powder keg that was the black community. Once again, a black male was killed by a white officer without consequence. It's truly hard not to see race as a factor in all of the aforementioned cases, especially this one. I cannot imagine a white police officer approaching a white 12 year old with the same force that was shown to Tamir. I've seen police show more restraint to whites with real guns who have recently shot or killed others, than what was shown to Rice.

The actions of the officer in the next case seem even more baffling. On April 4th, amid all the outrage, protests and waiting for justice of the previous year's shootings, a North Charleston, SC man, Walter Scott, was killed by the police. 33 year-old Michael Slager was responsible for the death of the 50 year-old black man.

This incident was also caught on tape, but the police didn't know the video existed immediately after the incident. The officer claimed that the victim, Scott, managed to secure his stun gun during a scuffle. Fearing for his life, the officer said that he shot Scott as the man charged at him with the electric device. Walter was struck five times out of the eight rounds that were fired.

Initially, the shooting was justified. Slager appeared to be the heroic officer defending the construct of law and order. His testimony was unchallenged and considered the unadulterated truth as with so many other officers. It was an open and shut case. Then the video surfaced.

Feiden Santana, the 25 year-old who recorded the incident was eventually called to testify in court. The video footage contradicted officer Slager's account. Instead of charging the officer, Scott was seen fleeing from the officer with his back turned before being gunned down. The Taser that he allegedly had lay behind the officer on the ground. Later, the officer is seen on tape placing the electronic gun next to Scott's lifeless body.

This video played out in the media again. The public was outraged by the blatant disregard of the law, evidence tampering and miscarriage of justice. Due to public pressure and video footage, Slager was charged with murder. This may have been the first national case where the officer was at least charged.

The first trial ended in a hung jury. Then, the federal government charged him with civil rights violations and he was returned to jail. Because of the mounds of evidence against him, Slager pled guilty to the federal case in exchange for the state's murder charge being dropped. In an unprecedented display of justice, Slager was sentenced to twenty years in prison.

The testimony of the cameraman Santana was very instrumental in Slager's demise. He stated under oath that he witnessed the officer chasing Scott until they reached the field. When he followed them, he found both men on the ground with the officer on top. Then Santana said that the officer punched Scott and stunned him with the Taser continuously. When Walter got up, and escaped the man's grasp, Slager shot him numerous times. "He was just trying to get away," Santana asserted (Channel14).

If it were not for the eyewitness testimony accompanied by the video, another corrupt officer would have literally gotten away with murder. The corruption charges for placing the weapon besides the deceased were also dropped as a part of the deal. In addition to the sentence, the Scott family was also awarded 6.5 million dollars in a civil suit. For once, justice was finally served.

The same would not be the case for Freddie Gray. About two weeks after Scott's death, the twenty five year-old black male died from injuries sustained during an arrest in Baltimore, MD. Gray's death sparked another round of protests and riots that led to the arrest of the officers involved. Eventually, all charges were dropped and the federal government neglected to bring charges.

On April 12, Freddie was arrested by police for allegedly possessing a knife. Just the very cause for the arrest raises suspicion. As many people, white and black alike, walk around with pocket knives and even daggers on their side, I have to question the police's motives in taking such extreme measures this scenario.

Logic notwithstanding, Gray was roughly escorted into a police van with handcuffs intact. During the transport, he sustained injuries that included a severed spinal cord. He was hospitalized and eventually died seven days later on April 19.

There is much speculation of what happened during that van ride. Popular opinion states that Gray was severely beaten and mishandled by police in the vehicle. Even eyewitnesses and video footage portray Gray's body being oddly limp before entering. Due to the fact that Gray initially ran from the police, doesn't rule out the customary beating that accompanies fleeing. Either way, a man had died in police custody and nobody was held accountable.

Eventually the outrage subsided. The family was paid a handsome sum of 6.4 million dollars. The police involved went back to work and filed their own lawsuit. The attempt was blocked by the federal government, and everyone went on with their lives. That is, until the next event occurred.

The next case flew under the radar for a while, until protest and slogans like "say her name," brought the incident to light. The death of Sandra Bland in the Waller County jail in Texas has yet to be prosecuted. On July 13, 2015 the 28-year old black woman was reportedly found in a semi-standing position in a holding cell. The official autopsy report ruled the cause of death was asphyxiation. The sheriff labeled it a suicide, saying that she hung herself with a trash bag.

It all started with a traffic stop three days earlier in Prairie View, Texas. The officer began following Bland for miles. The officer, trooper Brian Encinia had a history of performing Texas' pre-textual stops, where officers stopped drivers for little enforced offenses, hoping to initiate searches and find something criminal. He had issued over 1,600 tickets within the previous year for minor offenses.

On this day, he accelerated onto Bland's bumper so fast that she switched lanes to allow him to pass. When she failed to signal, the officer pulled her over. Visibly and understandably irritated, she responded as such when the officer alerted her to why she was being stopped. She informed him that the reason she changed was because of his closeness. Despite her protest, she was still given a ticket by the overzealous officer. Dash cam video shows the exchange between officer and citizen that escalated quickly.

"Do you mind putting out your cigarette," the officer asked, while writing the ticket.

"I'm in my car, why do I have to put my cigarette out," Sandra nonchalantly answered, well within her rights.

"Well you can step on out now," Encinia replied instantly and authoritatively.

"I don't have to step out..."

"Step out of the car," the officer interrupted with more force.

The officer then commanded her once again, while opening her car door. Sandra responded by asserting her rights.

"No, you do not have the right to open my door."

"I do have the right now step out of the car or I will remove you," the man yelled, obviously irate because of the woman's rightful defiance.

"Oh you gonna remove me for a simple ticket. Okay, let's do this."

The officer began to pull and pry without success. Bland protested, telling the officer not to touch her. The officer, visibly frustrated by now continued to reach into Bland's vehicle, assaulting her.

"Get out of the car. You are now under arrest," Encinia now screamed.

"Under arrest for what," Sandra countered, still refusing to budge.

The trooper didn't answer because he couldn't. Sandra had done nothing worthy of being arrested. His only response was to get on the phone, call for backup, and keep pulling on Sandra, to no avail. Disappointed, he pulled his Taser from his belt, pointed it at the woman, and demanded that she exit.

"Get out of the car or I will light you up!"

Under the threat of more violence, Bland exited the vehicle. The two moved off camera where Bland continued to complain. The officer instructed her to put her phone down and put her hands behind her back. She still asked why she was being arrested while the cuffs were being placed.

The officer had no answer. The two continued to argue back and forth. Bland complained about how the officer was handling her and stated that he was about to break her wrist. The argument continued with the officer screaming stop resisting. Then, you hear a scuffle where Bland was apparently slammed to the ground.

"Oh, so that make you feel like a man. You gonna slam my head into the ground! I got epilepsy motherfucker," Sandra whimpered.

"Good," was the man's cold response (Wall Street1)!

Then, the video ended. Bland was taken to jail where she stayed for three days. Footage showed her during that time making several phone calls in good spirits. Three days later she was dead.

An investigation ensued. The jail's version of events was upheld. They were not responsible for Bland's death. However, they were found to have not kept good surveillance in making their rounds. Also, the arresting officer was charged with perjury because of his version of events. He said he was in fear for his life, which the camera footage disproves.

Once again, in an indirect admission of guilt, Sandra's family received 1.9 million dollars in a wrongful death suit. The hashtag slogan, "say her name," emerged in an effort by activist to never forget her death. Considering my experiences behind the enemy lines of jail confinement, I know that there was more to what happened. Even the family and other parties believe that the county is involved in a cover-up.

Last year, a new video surfaced from Sandra's cell phone. It showed her view from inside the car. One gets a chance to really see the officer's aggressiveness. If you haven't seen the full video, I suggest you stop now and take a look.

The new video urged me to look more into who Sandra was. When I looked at her Youtube and social media pages, I began to understand why she was possibly killed.

She was very pro-black and anti-racism. She had numerous videos advocating for social justice and condemning white supremacist views. She was very active and outspoken in the community, just as she was in her car. She knew who she was, and knew her rights and wasn't afraid to let her voice be heard. Unfortunately, she articulated her thoughts to the wrong officer who couldn't handle it

The case of Bland and Scott are examples of how officers can perjure themselves in attempts to cover up wrongs. Freddie Gray's death is also an instance where police can concoct a scenario to protect their actions. Rice's death was just an outright vicious murder of a young kid that went unprosecuted. With these events all caught on camera, it seems like these happenings would cease. However, they just served as catalyst for more death.

Chapter 17

Alton, Philando, Korryn, Terrance

The deaths in the previous two chapters are only a fraction of the police misconduct and brutality that occurred throughout those years. With all of the public outrage and media coverage, one would think that the senseless killings of unarmed black men would have come to a cease. However, 2016 would see many more cases of murders caught on video.

On consecutive days in July, 2016 two more videos shocked the nation. The murders of Alton Sterling and Philando Castile were also filmed. The footage showed the outright aggressive nature of police towards black men even when they were cooperative and non- threatening. Unfortunately for them, the precedent was already set in previous trials, acquittals and grand jury decisions. No matter how clear cut the evidence the police were justified by law in their actions.

The first of these back to back killings was the death of Alton Sterling. The 37 year-old father of five, was killed in cold blood in Louisiana by two Baton Rouge police officers. Alton was standing in front of a convenient store, where he sold C.D.'s, with the permission of the store owner. It was here that Alton was approached by the police.

The officers came up to Sterling as his customer was leaving. One grabbed him by the back of the neck and told him not to move. Visibly surprised, Alton asked the officers what the problem was, while he attempted to turn around to face the officer who had him by the throat.

"What I do, officer. What I do," Sterling pleaded while being pushed towards a car in the parking lot.

"Don't move, stop moving," said the officer who had him in his grasp.

While Alton was struggling to find the problem, the other officer pulled his weapon and pointed at the face of the man. The anger, vigilance, and hatred were evident in his voice as he threatened to take the man's life.

"Don't you fucking move, or I'll shoot your ass in the fucking face! Put your fucking hands on the car! Put your hands on the car or I'm a shoot you in your fucking head! You understand me! Don't you fucking move or I'm a shoot you in your fucking head! You hear me! Don't you fucking move," the officer screamed loudly with the gun to Alton's face as he was being pressed against the hood of a civilian's car by the other officer.

"Alright, hold up, hold up, man! You're hurting my arm. I'm saying, what happened man?

Hold up, man my hands is on the car," Alton pleaded.

"Watch out," the officer with the gun instructed his partner as they both backed up from Sterling. No sooner than the Alton straightened up, the gun wielding man gave the command.

"Tase his ass!"

The other officer complied by executing the electric gun in Alton's direction. The man's body stiffened as the current entered into him. His hands froze out to his side.

"Get on the ground," the gun holder commanded. Stunned, Alton just stood with his hands up. "Hit him again, Ollie!"

The officer deployed the stun gun again. Alton went down to one knee from the impact. After the shock, the man stood up again, only to be rushed by the officer with the gun and tackled to the ground. A brief scuffle ensued with the officers on the man's back, trying to get his arms behind him. Then, the words that have been used to justify these killings were uttered.

"Gun... gun...gun!!"

Six shots were then fired into the defenseless, unarmed man. Alton Sterling was dead within moments. The officer continued to stand over Alton with the gun pointed at his lifeless body as he rifled through his pockets.

"You stupid motherfucker," the killer kept repeating, as he ravaged the dead body. He then asked his partner where the alleged gun was. His partner responded that he had taken it to the police car (CBS News).

After an investigation, the grand jury sided with the officers, stating that the shooting was justified. However, the police chief did state that one officer didn't follow de-escalation protocol and one did. The one who didn't was fired and the other was suspended for three days. Still no charges were brought.

Most disturbing about this incident was the officer's initial rage and aggression. It seemed that he was bent on killing Sterling from the start. He never stated why he was there or the nature of the problem when Sterling questioned him. The officer had his gun out from the beginning and started threatening to shoot the man within seconds of engaging.

Even the store owner came to Alton's defense, saying that he had sold merchandise outside of his store for two years without incident. Bystanders confirmed that Alton's hand was not reaching in his pocket at the time he was killed. Unlike previous cases, Baton Rouge rejected a $5 million settlement to the Sterling family and the case is still in litigation.

A black man in possession of a gun has always seemed to be a threat to police. Whether it's holstered, in a glove box, in his home, or on his seat, to possess a firearm is an instant death sentence to some. Alton had a gun and didn't disclose it to police. Many would say that is why he's deceased. However, this next instance will prove that even if you are licensed to carry, and inform police you have a weapon, you are still perceived as a threat.

On July 6, just hours after the video of Sterling's murder was released, 32 year-old Philando Castile and his girlfriend Diamond Reynolds were pulled over for a traffic stop in Saint Paul, Minnesota. The officer, Jeronimo Yanez, radioed in before the stop and said that Castile looked like a robbery suspect. Within forty seconds of the encounter, Philando Castile would be dead.

Castile told the officer that he had a licensed permit and a firearm in his possession after being asked for his license and registration. The eleven year school nutritionist thought he was being proactive. However, because of the trigger happy, prejudiced officer, his confession was his death warrant. The officer immediately got on the defensive.

"Don't reach for it then. Don't pull it out," Yanez commanded unnecessarily.

"I was reaching for, I, I…" Castile nervously explained.

"Don't, don't, don't pull it out," the officer said again while removing his own gun from the holster.

"I'm not pulling it out…" Philando again tried to explain. By now the officer had the gun pointed inside the car.

"Don't pull it out it out!"

"I'm not pulling it out, Castille again clarified.

"He's not pulling it out," his girlfriend tried to assure.

"Don't pull it out," the officer yelled before firing seven shots into the driver side of the car.

Five of the bullets hit the man, two piercing his heart. The officer stayed with the gun trained on the mortally wounded man. The girlfriend, Ms. Reynolds, immediately started recording a Facebook livestream. The next exchange sums the plight of many who've lost their lives in similar situations.

"I told him not to reach for it! I told him to get his hand open," the officer screamed with the gun still pointed.

"You told him to get his I.D. sir, and his driver's license sir," Reynolds said calmly. "Please don't tell me my boyfriend just went like that."

The video continued with police ordering the girlfriend out of the car along with her two year old daughter who was in the back seat. The woman was told to get on her knees before she was handcuffed and placed in the backseat of the cruiser. The footage ended with Ms. Reynolds breaking down right after the infant said, "it's okay mommy" (CBS Evening News)!

Castile's death echoes a common theme of police fearing for their life when encountering black men. The officer stated that when Castile was reaching for his wallet, the grip of his hand was too wide to be doing so. He had to be reaching for the gun. Listening to the video of the dead man's voice and his sincerity, he was no doubt reaching for his wallet, but unable to articulate it due to the officer's fear and constant interruption.

A year later, the officer was found not guilty of second degree manslaughter and two counts of dangerous discharge of a firearm. The officer had the audacity to use the fact that they were smoking weed in front of a little girl as a sign that he wouldn't bother shooting a police. As usual, they criminalized the victim by focusing on his past marijuana use and a small amount of weed found in the car. The usual indirect admission of guilt was given to the family of Castile in the form of a three million dollar settlement.

Less than a month after Sterling's and Castile's death, a twenty three year-old Baltimore woman would also die at the hands of police. Korryn Gaines, and her five year old son Kodi, were both shot after a six hour standoff with police at her apartment. The son survived but Gaines succumbed to multiple gunshot wounds and expired at the scene.

Ms. Gaines believed in what many called sovereign citizenship. This meant that she did not adhere to the governing laws of the state. She did not register her car, possess a license, and defied many other laws and ordinances that she believed to be oppressive. It was this belief that caused her to be stopped earlier in March for not having a license plate.

This incident was recorded on camera by Korryn, who was very boisterous and forthright with her attitude towards police. She stated that the police had no authority to detain her and explained that she did not participate in this system. She constantly told police not to harm or threaten her, and warned her son not to do anything the police ordered. She remained defiant to officers throughout. When the officers took her keys, ordered her out of the car and called for a tow truck she stood her ground.

"You're not gonna kidnap me. I've never been arrested. I haven't committed a crime. There is no victim here. If you put your hands on me, I promise you, I will haul your ass in that department right there," Korryn informed.

"Ma'am, just get out of the car. I've given you all these chances…," the cop explained.

"A chance to do what, sir, you're trying to steal my car. You're telling me that if I don't get out of the car, you're going to kidnap me and probably kidnap my children. It's not gonna happen. If you planned on shooting somebody today, you gonna get your wishes. I promise you, you will have to murder me. So go ahead and get ready to do that" (Cameragodz)!

The video continued with Gaines discussing other videos of police shooting black men. Her interpretation of the situation may seem extreme, but in the eyes of her and many others it was true. The police towing her car; is nothing more than it being stolen by the state. The police threatening to take her to jail; is also kidnapping. Nevertheless, she was given the tickets and made to leave her car.

At one point an officer admitted he knew Korryn Gaines. Apparently she had been in this position before. In fact, during the exchange, Gaines mentioned that she was in the midst of a lawsuit with the police and Eastern Correctional Institute. The familiarity may have been instrumental in her death.

Korryn was charged with disturbing the peace and failure to register a vehicle. Because of her stance, she didn't appear at the court date. A subsequent warrant was issued for her arrest. On August 1, 2016 officers came to the apartment of the 23-year old.

Upon entering, they found Gaines with a shotgun, and then retreated. That is when a six hour standoff occurred, in which Korryn again took to social media to record the events. She can be seen talking to her son, sitting on the floor with a shotgun, while police attempted to negotiate.

This is where the sequence of events got blurry. One report says that as officers entered Korryn fired the shotgun, which prompted the officers to return fire. Another version is that the officer's fired a warning shot. Korryn returned fire and was killed by the barrage of bullets that ensued. The more probable theory, which was proved in the settlement, is that the police got tired of her resistance and went in to end the matter once and for all.

The young black woman was killed inside of her domain. Furthermore, her five year old son was shot in the face. Gaines death exposes how police are less likely to use restraint when dealing with a person who is very vocal about their disdain for police or the American way of life; i.e. Sandra Bland.

The officer that killed Ms. Gaines was exonerated. The courts awarded her son 32.5 million and her infant daughter 4 million dollars in damages. However, the judgement was later overturned. The judge stated that it could not be determined from the autopsy and forensics if Ms. Gaines was lifting her shotgun when the officers fired, so it was no way of knowing if the shooting was justified or not. The courts erred on the side of caution and ruled it was.

Just a month and a half after Korryn's less publicized death, another video rocked the nation. On September 16, 2016, 40 year-old Terence Crutcher was shot in cold blood in Tulsa, Oklahoma. The shooting death of a black man and justification by the judicial system would once again play out and cause outrage in the eyes of the American public.

Apparently, Crutcher's car had stalled in the middle of the street. Police received calls about the vehicle being possibly abandoned. They arrived to find Crutcher tending to his disabled car. The first officer, Betty Jo Shelby, radioed for backup, specifying that the man was not cooperating and refused to show her his hands.

The video footage disputes this claim. The overhead camera of the helicopter and police cruiser dash cameras show Terence walking with his hands up in the direction of his vehicle. The tape also shows four other officers arrive, with their guns drawn and trained on the man with his hands up. As Terence neared the vehicle, the helicopter's audio illustrates the mindset behind the senseless shooting.

"This guy is still walking, not following commands," one man said.

"Time for Taser I think," his counterpart answered.

"I got a feeling that's about to happen."

"That looks like a bad dude too. He must be on something" (Wall Street Journal2).

A few seconds later, Crutcher goes down. The men in the helicopter, thinks he was just stunned. However, the shooter, Betty Jo Shelby confirmed over the radio that shots were fired. As her partner had already engaged his electric gun, subduing Terence, the woman felt it necessary to shoot to kill the man.

Police say that Crutcher was reaching inside the vehicle for something. Critics of the video often dispute that claim. Although PCP, a hallucinogen was found in the vehicle and in Crutcher's system, the video showed him presenting no viable threat to police.

As usual, the police used the presence of drugs to invoke the fearful excuse. Shelby was charged initially with manslaughter but was found not guilty of even the lesser charge of unlawfully and unnecessarily shooting Crutcher. Additionally, a wrongful death suit was dismissed by a federal judge on a technicality. The family has filed a second suit, which is currently pending.

With all four examples of this chapter, no officer was held liable for the death of the victims. The courts and the media took the focus off the actions of officers and instead put the deceased individual on trial. In each instance, the character, past, or habits were pushed to the forefront as a reason that the police were justified in their killings.

Alton's criminal record was constantly brought into play. Philando and his girlfriend's minor possession and use of marijuana were consistently flaunted in the news. Mugshots of the girlfriend were shown when she was detained after the murder. Korryn Gaines minor traffic violation and her boyfriend's outstanding warrant were used as focal point of the investigation. Finally, we see that Terence's usage and possession of a drug was used to make him an intimidating factor towards police.

This criminalization of color is reminiscent to the tactics mentioned in the first few chapters. Since the days of slavery, the black codes, reconstruction, and Jim Crow, the establishment has always used the propaganda that blacks were criminal and dangerous to excuse the treatment they received at the hands of the court and police. As we see from these modern day circumstances, little has changed.

These previous three chapters have only highlighted twelve of the thousands of less publicized police killings. Time, nor space, would permit me to examine and isolate each instance of police brutality and aggression towards black people. However, the pattern of police misconduct and judicial justification has been established in these in all other cases.

From 2016 to 2019 nearly 1000 Americans were killed by police per year. To keep from beleaguering the point, I will fast forward to the present year, 2020. In the midst of a pandemic, the cycle continued. Five more cases garnered the nation's attention at the pinnacle of a global shutdown.

Chapter 18

2020

On May 5th, 2020 while the country and most of the world were in the throes of uncertainty due to the Covid-19 virus, a familiar epidemic once again reared its ugly head. The disease of police brutality would be diagnosed through the videoed death of Ahmaud Arbery. The horrific execution of the 25 year-old African American "jogger" was broadcast to the world.

On February 23rd, the Brynn County Georgia man was accused of trespassing on a new construction home. Two "Karen" type individuals called the police and reported that Ahmaud was possibly casing the site. However, later footage emerged of several other visitors to the house who were not suspected of committing a crime.

Nevertheless, the father and son team who murdered him were dispatched. The video starts with Ahmaud running towards the parked truck in the middle of the street. The father, who is a former police officer, stood in the middle of the street with a shotgun. Arbery attempted to run around the man to the other side of the truck.

When he realized he couldn't get away, he ran toward the man who was pointing the gun.

That's when he was first shot in the chest. The wounded man continued to fight for his life, struggling with his assailant over the gun. In the midst of the affray, Arbery was hit with two more shotgun blasts, sending him staggering a few yards away where he fell to his death in the middle of the street.

A closer look at the video shows Ahmaud was visibly tired, when he was cornered by the men. Later reports indicate that the men had chased Arbery around the neighborhood for at least four minutes. The video was recorded by a neighbor who joined the chase, helping to trap the doomed man and seal his fate. Having nowhere to run, the helpless prey decided to engage the predatory shooters (News4Jax).

Within a couple of days, the district attorneys in the area decided no charges would be brought against the father and son team. The shooting was ruled a justifiable homicide. It was only after a local lawyer leaked the cell phone footage that caused national outrage were the trio of men arrested. Travis and Gregory McMichael, along with the trailer, William Bryan were all charged with malicious murder, felony murder and two other crimes within days of the video's release.

The fact that it took 74 days to arrest the men responsible for Arbery's death is very telling. If it had not been for the video exposure, Ahmaud's death would have gone unprosecuted and unnoticed. This is an example of how people in small towns, with political and judicial connections can commit crimes like this with impunity. In 2020, a cover-up reminiscent of 1940 KKK killings almost succeeded.

Another video surfaced that gives credence to why the Glynn County police and judicial system would ignore Arbery's murder. In 2017, police approached Ahmaud on his day off while he was in a local park. Police officers wanted to search him for weapons and search his car for drugs.

This angered Arbery and he became belligerent with officers. He told them that he works and he was in the park on his day off. He refused to let them search his car and stood his ground. He reprimanded police for targeting him and suspecting him of criminal activity. At one point, he became so disturbed that the police attempted to stun him, but the weapon didn't go off. He was handcuffed on the ground and eventually let go, walking off leaving his car in frustration.

This video, like all the others, was used to criminalize Arbery just days after the video surfaced about his death. However, this also may be why police and the county may have had a vendetta against him because of his attitude towards them in that situation. As I explained in my own experiences, cops, judges and prosecutors are capable of holding grudges and taking revenge on those who don't adhere to them or don't take their abuse of authority kindly.

Arbery's death sparked more riots and protests around the country. A hashtag, "I run with Ahmaud," was circulated and people vowed to run 2.23 miles in his honor, for the day he was killed, February 23rd. The majority of the population didn't know at the time, that Ahmaud wasn't out for a friendly stroll, but was running for his life, while being hunted like a prey. This case is still in litigation, but judging from previous examples, the three murderers will probably be released.

Approximately a week after Arbery's death and long before the video was released a Louisville, Kentucky woman was shot by plainclothes police officers as she lay in her bed. Probably because there was no video of the shooting, the case didn't garner that much national attention for a while. However, with the exposure of Arbery's murder, the case gained traction. The hashtag of "say her name," made popular in the case of Sandra Bland, was reborn.

On March 13, 2020 white officers, Jonathan Mattingly, Brett Hankinson and Myles Cosgrove entered the apartment of Breonna Taylor and her boyfriend Kenneth Walker at approximately one a.m. in the morning. The policemen were executing a now infamous "no-knock warrant," which gives them permission to barge into a residence without announcement. The warrant was supposedly for a person who no longer lived at the apartment.

Alarmed, Mr. Walker, who was a legally registered gun owner, grabbed his firearm. Suspecting that the police were intruders, he fired a warning shot in defense of his home. In response, the officers, who did not announce themselves, fired thirty-two rounds into the bedroom through a window and patio door. Mr. Walker was uninjured. However, the 26 year-old emergency room technician Breonna Taylor was killed when six of the bullets entered her slumbering body.

Initially the boyfriend, Mr. Walker was arrested for attempted murder. He was subjected to jail or home confinement for nearly two months before being released. As usual, the police attempted to criminalize him, Breonna, and her ex-boyfriend as being a part of a drug ring. Months after the shooting, Mr. Walker broke his silence and told his version of what really happened.

Although Taylor's death was ruled a homicide by the coroner, no charges were filed against the police. The self-handled investigation ruled the officers were justified in their use of force, like so many before them. This decision caused the usual outrage and protest sprang up in Louisville and around the nation in Breonna Taylor's name.

With the pandemic and the subsequent cases that were caught on tape, much pressure was placed on the Louisville Police department to bring charges. On September 23rd, the grand jury indicted only one of the officers, Hankinson. A slap in the face to Taylor's death, the officer was charged with three counts of wanton endangerment. The charges stemmed not from her death, but due to the bullets that entered the domain of the white family who stayed next door. Charges of homicide were never presented to the grand jury in regards to Taylor.

Instead of justice for the family, the state of Louisville agreed to pay Taylor's family 12 million dollars. This was the largest payout ever to the family of a black woman. However, it was given before charges were ever brought against the officers. This was a tell-tale sign that the officers would go unpunished.

At the height of the Arbery and Taylor discussions, the shot heard and seen around the world rang out. On May 25, the video of a police officer kneeling on a black man for eight minutes and forty-six seconds until he died shook the airwaves. 46 year-old George Floyd of Minneapolis, Minnesota died of asphyxiation while in police custody at the hands, or knees, of Officer Derek Chauvin in front of the entire world.

The police where initially called on Floyd for allegedly using a counterfeit $20 dollar bill to buy cigarettes. The store owners stated that he was visibly drunk and out of control. However, when police arrived, they found George and a passenger sitting in his jeep totally calm.

One officer approached the driver side. After about a minute, the officer pulls his gun for a second then re-holsters it. He proceeded to snatch Floyd out of the car, place handcuffs on him and lead him to the sidewalk. Floyd sits on the sidewalk while being questioned. The surveillance video still shows him extremely calm and cooperative.

The trouble started when the officers tried to lead Floyd to the back of the police cruiser. When he got to the car, the 6'4", 230-pound man went limp and fell to the ground. He informed police that he was claustrophobic and didn't want to be enclosed in the small space.

At this time, another team of officers arrived and assisted in trying to get George in the car against his will. While the four man team struggled, the final backup arrived. This is when officer Chauvin, and his partner Tou Thao, joined the affray. By this time, the officers had gotten the handcuffed Floyd into the backseat but he was still struggling in a horizontal position.

At this point, officer Chauvin steps around to the other side and pulls Floyd out of the car and drags him to the ground. Shortly after, the video shows three of the officers kneeling on the man's body; one on his legs, one on his torso, and Chauvin with a knee firmly planted on the man's neck.

At first, Floyd is quiet. Within a matter of minutes he starts pleading with officers to let him up. His cries of not being able to breathe went unheeded. Bystanders began to plea with officers in Floyd's defense. Officer Thao stood guard like a sentry protecting the onlookers from getting a clear view. A few approached closer before Chauvin pulled his mace and threatened to spray causing them to retreat.

One recorder was even told to move away and stop recording. Fortunately, another bystander pulled out their phone from a different angle. George begins to frantically beg for his life, as Chauvin appears to apply more pressure. The look of unconcern on his face his haunting as the large black man cries for his "mama" before going silent forever.

Sometime during the killing, police radioed EMS for a level two assistance. The problem was stated as blood coming from his mouth. Minutes later, they called again, for a level three emergency. However, even while Floyd lay motionless, no officer attempted to render medical treatment to him. Floyd showed no signs of life when the paramedics showed up.

In the aftermath of the video, the usual protest, outrage and rioting ensued. Initially police stated little about the death and made no arrest. After the video spread worldwide, and protests around the nation turned violent, Minneapolis finally arrested Chauvin and charged him with third degree murder. The charges were later upgraded two second degree and three other officers were charged with aiding and abetting within a month.

With the arrest, the public outrage quelled a bit, but the media onslaught on George's character and the police's innocence started. News stations and articles focused on George's criminal history and the reported drugs and alcohol in his system. Police advocates defended the knee tactic that was banned in many states except Minnesota. Nevertheless, the hold is not be used unless the subject is actively resisting. It is clear from the video that Floyd was not.

As of today, the case is dormant. There is still the question if justice will be served in the death of another black man. Or will the eyes of lady justice remain blind to the overzealousness of those with badges and rule their actions justified. As of today, officer Chauvin is out on a 1 million dollar bond. The trial date is set for some time in March. Hopefully, the outcome will not spark another uprising similar to the ones we had earlier this year.

Just when the storm was quieted in the Floyd matter, the killing of Rayshard Brooks hit the screen. The 27-year old black man was shot twice in the back by Atlanta police. The video shows a scuffle in which Brooks reportedly ended up with the police's stun gun and began to flee. Officers stated that he turned and pointed the gun, which caused officers to fire. He died hours later in surgery.

On June 12, Mr. Brooks was found asleep in the parking lot of a fast food restaurant. When the officers aroused him and he exited the car, the video shows he was visibly intoxicated. After a back and forth conversation with police, he agreed to take a breathalyzer. When the test indicated a positive result, the officers attempted to handcuff him.

That's when the scuffle ensued. The officers failed to subdue Mr. Brooks and he disengaged from them with the Taser in his possession. The officers gave chase and moments later, Mr. Brooks was shot in the back. "I got him," was the words from the officer as Brooks hit the ground (11Alive).

Unlike past cases the officers were charged within five days. Officer Garret Rolfe was charged with felony murder, aggravated assault, violation of oath and damage to property. His partner, Devin Brosnan was charged with aggravated assault and violation of oath. The grand jury ruled that the stun gun Brooks possessed posed no danger to the officers. Both officers were released on bond, one receiving nearly a half a million dollars from donors on his behalf.

These last four examples have been somewhat glossed over. The cases are still fresh and the public has had a much wider exposure to these deaths recently. The videos are still widely circulated and new perspectives are still emerging. Most importantly, the cases are still in the midst of litigation. The mystery is whether justice will be served.

I've only outlined about sixteen police involved deaths in this book. The reason is to show the consistency and patterns of these types of instances. A black man is killed by police. The victim is vilified in the media. The killing is justified by police and legal entities at first. The public is outraged, and protests ensue. Sometimes, a symbolic arrest is made to quell the anger. After court proceedings the officer is either acquitted or given a slap on the wrist. More outrage occurs before the family gets a settlement. There is reconciliation and pacification of the black community. Then all is calm, until the next shooting happens.

There are many more shootings that can be examined. The 2018, murder of Stephon Clark in Sacramento, where officers chased him into his backyard, firing 20 times, mistaken his cell phone for a gun, caused outrage. In September of the same year, off duty Dallas police officer Amber Guyger shot 26-year old Botham Jean, as he sat on his couch; claiming that she entered the wrong apartment and thought Jean was a burglar. Surprisingly Guyger was convicted of murder and received a sentence of ten years.

More recently, on August 23, 2020, a police shooting in Kenosha, Wisconsin ignited riots. 27-year old Jacob Blake was shot 7 times in the back in front of his children. He reportedly tried to break up a fight between two women, and when the police arrived, he was penned as a suspect. After a brief scuffle with police, they fired upon the unarmed man. Miraculously, he survived and no officers were charged.

Even as I conclude this chapter on November 5, 2020, another police involved death is in the headlines. On October 27, a little more than a week ago, 27 year old Walter Williams was killed in Philadelphia, PA. The mentally ill man was gunned down with several gunshots in front of his mother while having an episode. This recent killing leads me to ponder if there is an end in sight.

From the beginning of this book, we have seen how the state and police have always been at enmity with the African male. As these examples show, not too much has changed since then. It seems as if the black man still has no rights that the white man, more specifically, the white police is bound to respect.

Chapter 19

Black Lives Matter

In the wake of the first wave of police killings several symbolic images, slogans and hashtags emerged to commemorate, memorialize and politicize the deaths of those killed. Athletes, entertainers and even a senator, former Black Panther Bobby Rush, donned hoodies in public to honor the first martyr in the movement, Trayvon Martin. What once was an article of clothing to shield one from the cold became a constant reminder of the cold blooded murder of a teenage kid.

Another motto, "hands up; don't shoot," gained popularity after the death of Mike Brown, who reportedly had his hands up in surrender when he was slain. Protestors marched with their hands up screaming Brown's last words in the face of police all across the nation. T-shirts and banners could be seen displaying the message all across the black diaspora. Young Mike's cries continue to be heard through those words every time they're uttered.

Eric Gardner's last pleas also became widespread in the wake of his death. "I can't breathe" constantly embedded the image of the 43 year old black father being choked to death in the minds of everyone who hears it. This battle cry experienced resurgence with the death of George Floyd earlier this year. "I still can't breathe" linked the two men together in martyrdom, while reminding the populace that things still haven't changed.

A few more sayings round out the list of the last eight years. "Say her name," was popularized by the death of Sandra Bland. However, it has been used to highlight the deaths of Korryn Gaines, Atatiana Jefferson, who was killed by Atlanta police in her home, Breonna Taylor and many other black females who died unjustly at the hands of police.

"I run with Ahmaud," was used all over social media as a tribute to Arbery's Georgia killing. "Defund the police," is now widely used as proponents advocate for less police resources that enable law enforcement to engage in radical, terroristic tactics like using military equipment to police civilian neighborhoods. Last, but not least, "justice for…" has been inserted before countless known and unknown victims of police homicide.

Over the course of time however, three words emerged as the consensus attitude towards the situation. This phrase has been solidified by people from all races, colors, creeds, classes and nations as the default rallying cry in response to police brutality. "Black Lives Matter" is now synonymous with the struggle for equality and racial justice on behalf of Africans in America.

Unbeknownst to most, there are two different perspectives at play. "Black Lives Matter," the movement, is grassroots. It sprang from the passion of the people on the front lines in the cities most affected by police brutality. This mantra was a cry and an appeal to those establishments that didn't hold black lives to the same standards as others. They screamed this on all levels, through protest in the streets, to forums at city and government meetings. Black lives mattering was the ideological catalysts that caused many people to act and fight for social equality and racial justice around the country.

In steps Black Lives Matter, the organization. In July of 2013, the nonprofit organization was started by three women after the popularization of the hashtag on which they founded their group. Initially, they seemed to be sincere about the desire to end the killing of unarmed black men. They organized rallies, attended protest, and spoke on a wide variety of issues in a vast array of locations.

Lately, they have been criticized by their tactics and even by their mission statement on their website. Some grassroots organizers have testified how BLM has come in and co-opted their movements and made them less effective. Some say they are only in it for recognition and use the deaths of black men as a catalyst for more funding for their agendas, which hardly ever mention black men anymore.

Some critics of BLM cite the large donations received from people who have no interests in black lives. Many believe this income influences the group to change the narrative and only make symbolic gestures and statements without accomplishing any real change. All they reportedly do is make noise, cause confusion and move on to the next hot issue.

Another drawback to some is the sexual orientation of the founding members. Two of the founders are reportedly members of the LGBTQ community. Some think it is this lifestyle that prohibits the group from being one hundred percent for black lives and leads them to insert their own personal agenda under the façade of fighting for black lives. A look at the rhetoric in the BLM's mission statement may give credence to this opinion.

In certain places in their manifesto, BLM speaks about providing a safe and inclusive environment for queer and transgender blacks, which are less than one percent of black lives. They also mentioned tearing down the traditional, narrow-minded heterosexual mindset of most black people and destroying the patriarchal status quo of

Western civilization. Lastly, they voice the desire to uphold and promote the single parent household led by women and promote the dismantling of the traditional family.

These principles, which have nothing to do with the death of black men, have somehow usurped the original intention of the organization. The phrase and the organization has become an empty shell of the bullet it once was. Though NBA players sport the phrase on their shoes, jerseys, and warmups; though zealous members paint the yellow letters in streets, parks and blacktops; though commercials, songs, and literature repeats the sentiments, the thought of black lives mattering falls on death ears. There has been no substantial growth from the beginning of the movement until now. Blacks are still being slain and officers are still being acquitted.

Why is this so? There is another faction that counters with pledges of their own. In response to the displeasure of black deaths, others seek to justify or belittle the plight by deflecting the attention elsewhere. The most common and insulting response to the cry of black lives matter was "all lives matter." This phrase continues to be the source of argument for those with opposing views on the value of black lives.

After the large outcry and coverage of the deaths people who saw know wrong with the way that blacks were treated by police grew tired. They abhorred the constant attention that the deaths received and wanted to be heard. These lowly thuggish black men were the topic of discussion and they couldn't handle the constant exposure of the ugly American system.

So they undermined the concept of the marginalized. Their cry was not to insinuate that all lives didn't matter, but to inform all who would listen, or care to listen, that our lives mean just as much as yours, so stop killing us. The "All Lives Matter," crowd still refused to see the point and remained disillusioned.

I once used these illustrations. Say you are at the hospital, and your family member is dying of stage four Cancer. All the relatives are around the bed, preparing for the imminent death, and saying their last goodbyes. All of a sudden, a nurse bursts into the room and screams, "Well, thirty seven more people in the hospital have Cancer too!"

While the nurse's statement rings true, it shows no respect or sympathy for the family dealing with the loved one on a death bed. That family should be understandably upset at the timing of the statement and lack of empathy by the nurse. The fact that other people have Cancer does little to help this family in their particular situation.

So it is when people respond to black lives mattering with such rigidity and indifference. On the flipside, I can understand where their disconnected viewpoint stems. I've been in towns fundraising, where I didn't see one black person besides myself all day. So, there are literally thousands or even millions who have never seen police brutality towards blacks, other than television. They don't associate with blacks because there are none around. Consequently, it is hard to be compassionate for those you have no knowledge of.

Another reason for the despondency concerning black men who die by the hands of police is that it hasn't happened to those who think it doesn't matter. There is no ongoing visible pattern of police genocide of those who oppose the movement. If the shoe were on the other foot, there would no doubt be the same amount of rage at these actions as exhibited by the present victims.

In the midst of the confusion, another passive aggressive opposition to the voices of blacks emerged. On December 20, 2014, two New York police officers, Rafael Ramos and Wenjian Liu, were killed in as they sat in their patrol car in Brooklyn. A year and a half later, Micah X, killed five police officers in Dallas, Texas. These two isolated incidents propelled what is now known as the "Blue Lives Matter" movement.

With no proof to the contrary, the public automatically presumed that these police killings were retaliation for the many black deaths caused by police. While this may hold some credence, it is well documented that both assailants in these attacks had severe mental issues. Nevertheless, the fire had been ignited and the push to fiercely prosecute and punish those who attacked police as a hate crime was born.

Just like with the previous counterattack, sides had to be chosen. If you're for black lives, then you're automatically assumed to be against the police, and vice versa. Support of one, brought ire from the other. Battle lines were drawn and allegiances were pledged.

It seemed to most, the leaders, power structure and media were on the side of the police. After the aforementioned deaths of the officers, the president addressed the nation. Flags were flown at half-mast. The acts of violence against police were vehemently condemned. The funerals were televised and the nation mourned.

The reactions to these deaths were understandable. No one wants to see those that swore to protect and serve being murdered in cold blood. However, one may ask where was all the condemnation, presidential support, and national mourning when hundreds of blacks were killed in cold blood? Any death, whether accidental, ruled justified, or unjustified, should be given the same consideration when a citizen dies unlawfully at the hands of police.

Throughout these movements, the main issue got lost. Kaepernick's kneeling became not a stance against police brutality and injustice, but disrespect to America, the military and the police themselves. The blue line flag became a symbol not for police safety and respect, but as a new confederate flag in the eyes of black people. With all media conversation, confusion, and debating factions, the unarmed murder of black men by police has taken a back seat.

What opponents of the black lives matter movement forget or neglect to understand is none of this occurs without the initial actions of police. There would be no need to counter with all or blue lives matter, because there would be no need for blacks to scream they matter. So in essence, these sayings, groups and proponents served and still serve one purpose; to take the attention and deflect from the real problem.

Nevertheless, whether its black lives matter the movement, or Black Lives Matter the organization, both have did little to curb the disproportionate rate of black murders by police. They also have done less in ensuring that those perpetrators are prosecuted to the fullest extent of the law. What they have done is bring awareness. However, awareness doesn't mean anything if those who are aware and are able to bring about change do nothing but make symbolic gestures and sympathetic speeches.

A serious issue must be addressed. All throughout this book, we have seen from the beginning of this country, until now a disdain for blackness by the state and particularly police. The abuse and brutality is much less covert and blatant than in earlier years but is still present. Police are still given leniency, permission and justification to do as they please to black men.

What does this say about them when they carry out their actions? Are they less human? Are they just following orders from higher ups? Does their upbringing and life experience give them a propensity towards this type of behavior? Are they suffering from post-traumatic stress syndrome? Or are they just a victim of a systematic racist entity that trains them to fear or dominate the darker man? Or, are they a combination of all these things. In this next chapter we will attempt to delve into the mindset of an officer, who will be so quick to kill, rather than protect and serve.

Chapter 20

A Thin Blue Line

Most Americans agree that being a cop, especially in this day and age is a difficult job. The mere fact that one has to go out in society and possibly deal with the most dangerous criminals and situations daily is gut wrenching. Imagine going into every call, knowing that you may not make it out alive. This fact alone can bring about all sorts of stress on the minds of the individuals that wear the blue uniforms and silver or gold badges.

Add to that, the other everyday problems of being an officer, and the mental instability increases. Just like any profession, you have job politics. Police are also underpaid in comparison to many career fields. They also endure pressures to make quotas, and arrests that lead to convictions. These requirements are normally essential to ensure advancements up the ranks in police departments.

Then, if you factor in the everyday problematic situations that regular people face, an officer is just one emotion away from an explosion. Police have to cope with things like financial instability, relationship problems, addictions, mental and physical health issues, low self-esteem, depression, PTSD, loneliness, shame, guilt, fear and a host of other issues. The law enforcement officer is not above the challenges and pitfalls that occur in the lives of all humans.

A combination of all of these factors, have a detrimental effect on the lives of police. They are known to have a high divorce rate in their marriages. Officers also have a higher rate of domestic violence incidents than regular civilians. Also, the stress of their occupation may lead them to seek out other vices. All sorts of addictions, from alcohol, hard drugs, prescription pills, gambling, prostitution and many other ills accommodate life as a public servant.

It is because of their mortality and subjection to human error, the person and position of police officer must be highly scrutinized. Not only because the safety of others depends largely on their ability to function properly. They must be examined even more so when the seemingly unnecessary deaths of others occur at their hands. Many different aspects of the makeup of the officer that kills unarmed citizens must come into play.

The main thing that must be addressed is the moral capacity and the mental state of the officer. It has been well documented throughout history and within this book that the majority of police murders are white officers killing black men. So one must ask, why aren't there more black officers shooting white men? Are they more moral and ethical than their white counterparts? The answer lies in the breakdown of their training; familial, societal, and professional.

Most children learn morals, values and their view of the world from their parents. Their parents learned from their parents and so on and so forth. As it relates to this subject, I am only a generation removed from a time where blacks and whites were systematically and socially separated. At 42 years-old, my 67 year old father attended a segregated high school in 1969.

Consequently, white police officers, who are my age, had parents who came of age during that time. Some older officers or administrators may have even experienced that era where blacks were considered less than equal firsthand. Either way, the men who are now officials, may have been directly or indirectly influenced and inundated with the attitudes of that time frame. Consciously or unconsciously, that innate mindset is prone to emerge in the performance of their duties.

White men who have been taught that blacks are not human or more criminal may be inclined to treat them as such under the power of their badge. White officers who have been separated or have had little to no contact with blacks may be persuaded by stereotypes and fear to overact in situations due to their lack of understanding. Lawmen who have bought into the ideological premise that blacks were the enemies of the earth may lean toward aggression when encountering them because of that preconceived notion.

Earlier in the book, the actions of Chief Darryl Gates of Los Angeles were highlighted. He was much maligned for recruiting rural southerners from Alabama, Mississippi, Georgia and other places to police the black neighborhoods of L.A. Because of this disconnect, that department became notorious for police brutality and other civil rights violations against black people. Today, the same problem exist where officers have no connection to and hold negative views of the people in which they are called to serve.

In addition to the upbringing, there are other social forces at play in regards to police and their treatment of blacks. The mainstream media, including television, movies, radio, news, internet and other outlets use their influence to paint blacks in a negative light. Whether the ultra-masculine, hyper-sexual, intoxicated rapper, the hardcore, heartless, violent drug-dealer, the shiftless, lazy pimp or thief, or the uneducated, buffoonish moron; songs, films, articles, and telecast make it easier for police to exercise prejudicial tactics in the handling of the black man.

No matter how partial an individual may attempt to be, those images have an overwhelming effect on one's perception. Therefore, illegal searching, profiling, unlawful arrest, unnecessary detainment becomes justified through loopholes written into the law books. For some officers, media is their only contact with blacks due to social, cultural, familial, and demographic separation.

In addition to the aforementioned influences, police training is also a detriment to public interaction in black communities. Cadets undergo a series of conditioning exercises to prepare them for life on the force. One is the MILO range exercise. This practice involves candidates engaging in firearm training in response to dangerous situations.

Police participate in simulations that require them to react to human interaction deciding when to use deadly force. This exercise requires split second decision making as images pop up. The officer must determine whether the image is a threat or not. They also grade on marksmanship, accuracy and timing.

In many of these scenarios, the dangerous targets are black men or dark images with guns pointing. Other images are white people who may be hostages or endangered targets. Subconsciously, this automatically programs them to see black people as a threat and white people as the ones to protect at all cost.

The drill is supposed to equip officers with the skills to judge when the use of firearm is needed or if a situation can be de-escalated without using a weapon. It reportedly teaches police to transition from pursuit, to contact, defusing the dangers of the situation at every step. However, as we see from years of proof, this only works in certain cases.

With the countless murders of unarmed and non-threatening black men, there is an obvious double standard evident in this training. We've all seen videos where white suspects run from police, fight or strike them, attempt to take their weapons, refuse to drop dangerous objects, disobey commands, fuss, curse, and act aggressively towards police. These acts seldom result in death. Contrarily, as soon as a black suspect moves wrong, the officer all of a sudden fears for his life, and deadly force is the only option. This may be a direct result of the MILO training.

Another source of the aggressive, kill first nature of some police is their military background. Many officers have served or may be trained by those who've served in military combat zones. Given the prevalence of PTSD in combat veterans, this condition is not foreign to police. When given a badge, it may be hard to separate a high stress dangerous situation where one is expected to protect, from a battle tested soldier who was trained to kill.

This theory is backed up by studies. The Marshall Project stated that officers who were deployed are 3 times more likely to fire their weapon on duty. Additional data suggest that 20 percent of police officers are military veterans (Marshall Project). So in essence, one in five police officers has a high potential of violence while on duty. Having one officer who is more prone to shoot because of war experience is too many, not to mention one in five.

I witnessed a prime example of this mindset when I was locked up for a probation violation in Virginia Beach in 2011. I was awaiting court with two veterans. One, Snipes, was serving his second term of two years for assault. He was a military sniper, hence his name. The other, Allen, was facing a four year sentence for a bevy of crimes. I listened to their dilemma as we sat.

"I just don't know what to do," Snipes complained. "I try to find a job, but it's hard. All I know how to do,is kill!"

"I know what you mean. It's not easy for me either. I hear Blackwater is hiring though," his counterpart said.

Blackwater is a mercenary group that contracts overseas for special missions. They are known for their brutality and were even the subject of a scandal for their actions in several parts of the Middle-East. The fact that these two young men under the age of twenty-five had such a hard time adjusting to regular life after one tour of duty, should make the government think twice about giving men like this guns and badges and releasing them into the community without proper restraint.

Another problem with the law enforcement system is the age and requirements needed to become police. Most academies require cadets to be twenty one years of age, but some start accepting candidates at eighteen. Other than having a G.E.D. or a high school diploma, the only other qualification is being able to pass a physical test. To my knowledge, there are no psychiatric, moral, ethical, or other serious mental evaluations that are necessary to vet potential officers.

Giving such power to someone so young and inexperienced is a danger to the development. Most people at that age have not matured enough to form their own opinions about life. That may make them susceptible to influence by views of older officers with power. Also, the young officers may do things to fit in or be "one of the guys," including taking on the attitudes and viewpoints of elders that are not conducive to good and fair policing.

Their age and experience notwithstanding, the new officer also faces his own inner demons. There are those who may have been picked on or bullied in school. They may have not been popular and left out of the social graces of the "cool kids." In this case, they may develop contempt for certain types of people and use their badges and position as a source of vengeance towards the people who hurt them vicariously through the people they encounter.

Then you have those that have never been in positions of power. These officers exhibit somewhat of a Napoleon complex; not in size, but mentally. They've never had control before and the slightest bit of resistance, is like a personal challenge to their manhood. It is then when you have seemingly innocent situations escalate to the point where someone ends up dead.

The last type of officer is the one who has straight up contempt or fear of black men. This officer let's his own beliefs cloud his judgment on how to proceed with dealing with citizens of opposite color. There is no remedy for this except his personal self-examination and change of heart, soul and mind. However, no matter how hard we try to sugarcoat the fact, there will always be men with evil contempt for those who don't look like them. The travesty is when they are supposed to serve and protect with those barriers to human decency in place.

I experienced this blatant disdain firsthand at the height of the unrest over police brutality in 2015. I was at a Planet Fitness in Virginia Beach. While working out I noticed a young white man on the machine a few feet away. He sported a Virginia Beach Police Academy shirt. When we locked eyes,

I nodded my head, while he kept a tight lipped, stern look on his face.

Feeling the tension, I decided to break the ice with lighthearted conversation. I asked was he a cadet, how long he'd been in the academy and did he like it. Each question was met with a slight nod, and the same fixed gaze. The more I tried to show friendliness, the narrower his eyes grew and the redder his face glowed. I knew then that this young white kid would rather be doing anything in the world other than talking to me at that moment. I wished him well and continued my workout.

The above mentioned issues with modern day police are not all inclusive. There are many more factors that cause police to overreact in situations that could be handled more civilly. This lists is just to make a point that all police are human and subject to human emotions, feelings, prejudices and biases that may cause them to error.

I also must note that these rogue cops represent only a minute faction of the law enforcement sector. Most officers are respectful of the badge they hold and the lives of their fellow citizens. The problem arise when these upstanding officials, go along with, cape for, excuse, cosign or look the other way when the small percentage of evil officers go awry. It is only then when the old adage holds true that "one bad apple spoils a bunch."

If a good officer sees his partner or a fellow officer breaking the law, violating the rights of citizens and disrespecting his oath to protect and serve, it should be their duty to report this behavior. They should be praised and rewarded. Unfortunately, the total opposite is true. Those whistleblowers are often ostracized, alienated, reprimanded, or targeted by their comrades. In extreme cases they are sometimes fired by the departments or found dead under suspicious circumstances.

This reluctance to discipline offenders leads to a bigger problem. Those who continue to get away with violations become more emboldened to commit more offenses. They develop the mindset that they are above the law. In many of the officer involved shootings, the perpetrator has a documented history of brutality, harassment, and violations that have gone unpunished. This immunity from correction ultimately leads to the unnecessary death of many.

The thin blue line extends even to officers who murder their peers. I am reminded of the 2006 murder of Officer Seneca Darden in Norfolk, VA. Darden was assigned to a plainclothes unit in a project of the city. While responding to a domestic disturbance, he had his gun out ordering a suspect to the ground.

At some point during this exchange, other uniformed officers arrived on the scene. One, white Officer Gordon Barry, noticed Darden and ordered him to drop his weapon. Darden turned around and before he could identify himself, he was shot multiple times by his fellow officer. He died shortly after.

Without asking questions like, "how did the other officers not know Darden was on location before they arrived," and other logical questions, one sees the main point of this book in action. White officer sees a black man with a gun. Officer sees him as a threat or criminal. Officer shoots with the intent of using deadly force. An innocent black man, in this case an officer of the law, is needlessly dead.

The Virginia State Police performed an investigation. As to be expected, the officer was cleared of any wrongdoing. The only person punished was Darden's partner. He was immediately fired because it was said that he was told not to go to the scene. It is my belief that he was discharged because he was ready to expose the reality of the situation that night and would not cooperate with his fellow officer's version of events in the death of his partner.

Nevertheless, a large funeral procession was held for the slain officer. His family received a $600,000 settlement, a small amount to compensate for the loss of a husband and a father. Even more disturbing, Barry, the killer, was allowed to stay on the force for two more years. In 2008 he resigned with a severance package of nearly $58,000 with an additional $20,000 to be paid to his lawyer. Even within the rank and file of the police department, a black man still has no defense or advocate against a white officer.

Most officers know that crossing that thin blue line between being an officer or standing up for what's right is a very costly thing to do. Because they've invested so much time, effort and passion into the career, few take that risk. With families, bills, lifestyles and images to uphold, the inevitable consequences for doing the right thing just aren't worth it. So people with righteous hearts sit idly by and watch, while savagery goes unchecked. As Edmund Burke said, "Evil triumphs when good men do nothing" (OpenCulture).

The silence of associates is not the only reason for the malady that exists from the blue line concept. The overall idea that the police officer is 100 % perfect in everything they do, completely moral, ethical, unbiased, and above reproach from anyone, allows these heinous acts to continue. The legal posturing, maneuvering, political filibustering, double talk, and the independent investigations that mostly yields favor to the offender, are all methods of upholding the faulty premise that officers are never to blame.

So until the courts, judges, and prosecutors admit that police are human, subject to error, anger, rage, spite, and vengeance, there will never be justice. Until other police stand up for what is right, people of color will continue to be oppressed, violated, and killed by white men with badges. Until America realizes and addresses all of the issues set forth in this chapter, rogue police will forever get off the hook when they err.

The question was posed at the beginning of the chapter. Why aren't there countless instances of white men and children being killed by black cops? Are they more ethical, humane, just, or compassionate? No. The reason is because black officers know that "white folks" will not tolerate it. By white folks I mean the ones in power. The same ones that ensure white officers get acquitted will be the same ones to assure that the black officer gets punished to the fullest extent of the law.

To end this one-sided phenomenon, there must be a reckoning. Black people have to cease being tolerant, excusatory and complicit in incidents where black life is lost in this manner. They must refuse to participate in the systems that perpetuate the reoccurring cycle of death. Blacks must adjust their viewpoint of the matter and realize that change starts at home.

Chapter 21

What must be Done?

So far, this book has laid out plainly the many problems of the judicial system, mainly the police, as it relates to black men. There is no point, however, in outlining a problem if there is no solution. Hence, this last chapter will focus on what has to happen in order to curb the senseless deaths of black men at the hands of police nationwide.

To start, blacks must focus on their own treatment of one another. Opponents of black lives matter, the movement, always bring up the fact that black men kill each other at a much higher rate than police do. While I always hated this rebuttal as it has nothing to do with the situation at hand or the despicable actions of police, there is some credence. How can we expect others to value black lives if we don't ourselves?

Not to excuse police murders, but when black men start respecting each other, standing up for each other, and protecting each other, the natural response of the outside communities is to reciprocate the action. It has long been said, to get respect, you have to give it and earn it. With the continuous fratricide within the ranks of black males, it is hard for white police to feel any sense of value when encountering us, which leads to a subconscious attitude of indifference towards black life. In short, when we constantly slaughter each other in the street, we indirectly give police permission to do the same.

Another cliché that I detest is "He shouldn't have resisted!" While resisting arrest, fleeing, not cooperating, and disrespect to police should not warrant a death sentence on sight, there is a level of culpability that has led to most shootings. Being that we know we are behind enemy lines when dealing with police, we should be aware of the trigger happy nature of some police and act accordingly.

I have always been opposed to "the talk" approach when dealing with police. This method is when you sit young or old men down and lay out the dos and don'ts of encountering the police. It was my opinion that encouraging citizens to be passive, submissive, and obedient in the presence of violations or unlawful stops was cowardly and emboldened police more. Assertiveness, firmness and dignified indignation have always been my approach.

Most recently, I was posed a question by friend and Goldsboro County Commissioner Bevan Foster that caused me to rethink my strategy. He asked, "How would you tell your son to act in the presence of officers in this current climate to ensure that he made it home?" This personal application caused me to change my viewpoint.

To answer the question, I would tell my son to remain calm. Don't give the officer any more information than necessary. If you're upset or frustrated, don't show it verbally or in body language. Be polite and relaxed. Don't act nervous or fidgety. Don't make any sudden moves. Look him in the eye with hands in sight. Most importantly, I would tell him to call me or somebody with the location and situation. If he could do so without being obvious or antagonistic, I would also tell him to record it.

As history has shown, this still doesn't guarantee the situation will go smooth. However, as my friend eloquently surmised, "they already have the loaded gun. There's no need to give them extra ammunition." As stated in Proverbs fifteen verse one, "A soft answer turns away wrath, but grievous words stir up anger." In other words, it is better to be quiet and go home, than speak defiantly and die.

Wisdom like that only comes from experience. Therefore, older men must take their rightful place in the community to help younger men cope with the realities of the times. There must be leadership and guidance that steers men away from encounters with police and towards life, liberty, the pursuit of happiness and longevity.

[301]

However the collective absence of leadership in the black community is another story for another time.

To avoid these situations, black men have to be more cognizant of acts that lead to encounters with police. Earlier, I examined the drug laws and how unfair, unjust, and excessive they are. However, if I and many of my peers were not involved in drug dealing, we wouldn't have been subjected to the stiff penalties. So even though the laws are wrong, we still have to take the proper responsibility for allowing them to be imposed on us.

The same applies with putting ourselves in positions where police have a reason to accost us. Whether selling loose cigarettes, resisting arrest, fleeing, domestic violence, or committing any other crime, we run the risk of a situation going wrong that could have been avoided. We, as a targeted species, must take every precaution how we move to make sure that no one has cause to get the police involved with our actions.

The previous stances I would've never taken before. They all have a feel of blaming the victim. They seem sort of precautionary or reactionary as it relates to police misconduct. Being that the goal is to prevent black deaths, however, anything that will keep men alive in the presence of police or help them avoid the dangers altogether is a welcomed solution.

There are some things we can do proactively. One of those is to police our own communities. This means that men and women will take the responsibility to enforce rules, standards, ethics, and codes of behavior that is to be expected and respected in their own environment. There will be a commission of people who impose penalties, restrictions and punishments on transgressors, using the police and judicial systems only as a last resort. In this way, encounters with police will be reduced as well as the chance for police induced shootings.

I experienced this concept on a recent visit to LA. On Sundays in the Crenshaw district, they have a festive like gathering near Leimert Park. There was food, music, dancing, vendors, art and thousands of black people out enjoying themselves eating and shopping. There were no incidents of violence and not even one argument or disagreement that I noticed.

The reason for this security was the presence of the men from the Nation of Islam. These black men had the streets barricaded off, organizing the jam packed event with efficiency and order. Just their sheer dominating authority warded off any potential threat to the peace and serenity of the event. In the heart of South Central where gangs and guns are prevalent, not a police officer was needed because strong, black men were able to take control of their community and protect the people entrusted to their care.

So this is what needs to happen all across the country. Strong black male leadership must band together in a show of unity and force. That not only will make members of our community respect us, but also people outside of the community will feel less empowered to disrespect us. When something happens in the neighborhood, instead of the police, one can call the groups like the Fruit of Islam or other groups that are less inclined to use force in dissolving the situations.

Now, the focus must shift to what has to happen on the other side of the coin. It is possible that all of the previous things can be done, and there will still be instances of police genocide towards the black race. Therefore, there are some very specific things that must be done by, for, and towards police to stop this longstanding trend. The first and foremost solution is to hold them accountable for their actions.

Accountability is a word often used, but seldom implemented. It requires discipline and a trusted outside source that will not allow a person to continue in the error of their ways. To hold a person accountable can be accomplished in a variety of methods. One of those ways is punishment. As it relates to police shootings, punishment is the only way to ensure that this phenomenon comes to an end.

It is obvious that police are more apt to shoot in non-life threatening situations because there are no repercussions. They always use excuses like, "I feared for my life," "I saw him reaching for something," "I felt like this...," or "I thought that." To date, these justifications have been enough to get officers off the hook, when lethal force is clearly not necessary. In turn, police are inclined to shoot more knowing they have an out.

In order to reduce the likelihood of police killing an unarmed person, every time this happens, the death penalty should be imposed. With this sort of law strictly enforced, we would see a drastic reduction in incidents like these in this book. Police would be more likely to be less aggressive, treat citizens they encounter with respect, and if force is necessary, shoot to disarm or injure, rather than to kill. Knowing their life is at stake, police would think twice before acting wantonly in certain situations.

Another change that would make a difference is ratio and residential proximity of officers in relation to the community they serve. As pointed out in the Ferguson investigation, it was found that the city's population was nearly half white and half black. In contrast, blacks made up less than twenty percent of the police force. This is a recipe for disaster as reports emerged of numerous cases of police brutality and civil rights violations that went unpunished.

This is an example of something mentioned earlier in the chapter. Many whites who are officers have no relation, connection, and may have contempt for blacks. Their attitude of disdain comes out in their work as views towards their victims may be negative. The feelings also may be mutual on the part of the black community where experience and history has exposed the animosity in years past. This makes for tense encounters whenever the two meet.

The second part of this issue is that the officers don't live in the neighborhoods they serve. This unfamiliarity is also a cause for suspicion, prejudice and fear when people and police interact. Since the officers have no vested interest in the neighborhood, they have no interest in the livelihood of the people that live there as well.

The solution to these problems is simple. The racial makeup of the towns and neighborhoods should also reflect the racial makeup of police officers and departments that serve those areas. It is human nature that people feel more comfortable and trusting around those that look like them and have similar experiences. They tend to relate and understand each other more. There would be much less misunderstandings. As it relates to this subject, a simple gesture or word won't be misconstrued as a life-threatening move and result in an unnecessary shooting.

Also, officers should live in the neighborhoods they serve. Their residing among the people promotes a sense of oneness, with the common goal of everyone chipping in to protect and serve the community. The familiarity with the residents will foster trust, faith and leniency on both sides of the equation. Just the mere presence of an officer in the neighborhood exudes security, especially if he has shown that he values the community and people who live there. The fact that he or she knows everyone and their family will make it less probable that he would take a life unnecessarily.

Another thing that must be done is the removal of rogue officers and those who have had consistent complaints. Just as Clinton's crime bill suggests, if an officer has more than two incidents where he has been found to have brutalized, harassed, violated or transgressed any citizen, he should be permanently relieved of his duties. Yes, if three strikes and you're out applies to regular citizens, how much more so should it apply to those we hold at a higher standard.

In order to prevent mentally instable, immature people from becoming police officers, there has to be a much more complex process put in place. Strenuous and in-depth mental evaluations should be conducted to ensure that they are psychologically fit to handle such a position. Their family history and adolescent school years should be investigated to uncover any possible trauma experienced early on. These assessments should be performed on a continual basis in order to detect the possibility of misconduct.

Police officers should also undergo a much more lengthy process to get the badge. Instead of a few months training academy, there should be a two or four year degree program. Just like lawyers, doctors, real estate brokers and the like, candidates should have to pass a state board test. If successful, then they should have to obtain a license, pay fees and require continuing education as does many other professions. If they break the code of ethics, they would be subject to probation or outright revocation depending on the severity or number of offenses.

There should also be strict, non-exceptional penalties for officers who conveniently have their dash or body cameras off during encounters. A no tolerance policy for this offense will result in immediate termination when complaints and violations are alleged. It does no good to have cameras if they are not utilized when needed.

Judicially, the courts and the police need to do away with the internal investigations. State, federal and government have also shown themselves to be partial. My solution is to allow a world organization to look at any event in which a citizen is harmed or killed by officers. There should be a non-partisan body like the United Nations minus a United States representative to examine all cases of death. Since other nations have loudly condemned the police and the U.S. judicial system in the handling of these matters, they would not hesitate to bring swift justice to offenders.

Another phrase, "defund the police," has also become very popular of late. This term does not mean doing away with the police altogether. It is simply a plea for the government to reduce the resources and numbers of police created by the 1994 crime bill. A cutback in officers and monies for departments will shorten the long arm of the law and siphon some of the powers that allow them to be above reproach and scrutiny.

Accountability, diversity, licensing, punishment, screening, and independent investigations all sound good in theory. The problem is getting those in power to really consider and implement these concepts. Unfortunately, so many people benefit from the corrupt criminal justice system and the laws thereof, it would be bad for business if these steps were taken.

So in essence, there has to be a complete dismantling of the system. This paradigm has shown itself to be one-sided and detrimental to minorities of all color, race, and ethnicity; but mostly to blacks. Even the unity, discipline, obedience, restraint from criminal activity and the self-policing mentioned earlier is a hard feat to accomplish. Therefore, many, including myself at times, have grown hopeless and grown to accept the status quo as a never ending reality.

As formidable as the challenge may be, America and its citizens must never give up on the creed that it was founded upon. The truth that all men are created equal must be achieved no matter what the costs. The life, liberty, and pursuit of happiness that the Declaration of Independence guarantees must be given to all. If not, the consequences of the latter part of the document must be executed; and the government must be altered or abolished and replaced with a new, more equitable institution.

The Conclusion

From the start of this book, until the finish, we have seen one common factor throughout. That is the unfair treatment of the black man by this American system of so-called justice and equality. Whether enslavement, slave patrols, slave codes, black codes, Jim Crow, segregation, CoIntelPro, drug conspiracies, crime bills, stop and frisks, racial profiling, and any other initiative, unjust laws have been enacted and upheld to criminalize the black man, thereby making it harder for him to exist. Throughout the centuries, with all of the technological and ideological advancements, for black men in America, the more things have changed, the more things have remained the same.

Some people may beg to differ. With the prosperity and notoriety of a few black men, there is an illusion of equality; a perception of a level playing field. If Jay-Z, P.Diddy, Will Smith, Denzel Washington and other entertainers can make it to multimillion dollar status, then everyone else could too. If Lebron James, Patrick Mahomes, Russell Wilson and other athletes can sign multimillion dollar contracts, then there are no excuses. Lastly, if Barack Obama, a bi-racial man, could become president, then racism must be dead in America.

This misconception could not be further from the truth. What many fail to realize is that for every Jay-Z there are 10,000 Freeway Ricky Ross's who didn't have the musical talent to escape the drug game. For every Lebron James, there are 50,000 Kaleif Browder's who lacked athletic prowess and got caught up in the system as early as 16 years of age. For every Barack Obama, there are 100,000 black children who are not privy to the trust fund education and fall victim to the everyday perils and pitfalls of life in low income areas.

To put it simpler, the success of a few black men in a minute sector of society, means nothing, if the rest of the population is stagnant or in regression. As stated earlier, there are more black men in prison, on probation or parole, than were enslaved at the end of slavery. This fact alone is evidence that America has made a concerted effort to target black men under the guise of law and order to continue the systematic enslavement of black men allowed through the exceptional clause in the thirteenth amendment.

Those who refuse to look at these truths fall into several categories. There are those who remain unaffected or untouched by the laws or repercussions of them. These would mostly be the white Americans who only hear about the disparities, injustices and violations through news broadcasts, articles, videos, or third party stories from their black friends. They remain insulated and while appalled or even outraged, they are reluctant to give up or sacrifice their privileged comfort to demand that change be implemented. They sympathize, empathize, or even protest, but rarely do anything to dismantle the system that continues to allow injustices.

Then, there are those who suffer from cognitive dissonance. These are people, mostly black who have made it out of the throes of the ghetto or have grown up around whites and people with money. They have never had to experience any of the unfortunate circumstances mentioned in this book. They tend to look down on those who suffer at the hands of the American system and blame the victims of a cruel reality. Even though they know things are not right, they ration away the injustices by focusing on their position in life, until the chickens come home to roost.

The most disparaging group is those that ignore the problem because they benefit from it. These are the professionals that work in the systems that perpetuate the crimes against black men. Whether politicians, judges, lawyers, prosecutors, jailers, sheriffs, court officials and administrators, prison workers, and many other positions, all are guilty in some shape, form, or fashion, when they see something wrong, but decline to stand up because it puts their livelihood in jeopardy.

There's the police officer who fails to report his partner for fear of being alienated. There is that prosecutor that ignores exculpatory evidence to gain favor with the judge. It may be that politician or city official that votes in favor of the group with the most money or influence. Or, it may be the mayor or Sheriff who sides with the police in order to get reelected. These are just a few examples of people who turn a blind eye to wrongdoing in order to receive a tangible benefit or remain secure in a position.

I am reminded of former California Attorney General and current Vice-President elect Kamala Harris. While I applaud her efforts and her representation of a minority woman who has risen to prominence, she is an example of those mentioned above. When asked about her history of incarcerating black men and women at an astoundingly high rate in California, she answered, "I was just doing my job. (Kimberley)"

That particular response says much about her and the overall system and position she held. The fact that locking black men and women up was a part of her job description is very much of the problem. Even more, her willingness to perform that aspect of her duties so ferociously was a major source of advancement for her career. That she ignored the damage that her tasks inflicted upon her own community in lieu of the favor garnered from her superiors is an example of everything that is wrong with the system. Those families that were destroyed were just collateral damage in the progressive symbolism that she now represents.

Not to single her out, this is a major issue across all walks of life. Former President Obama also failed to directly address the issue of police brutality during his eight year presidency. His fear of upsetting mainstream America and the police by outright condemning police misconduct led to a silent endorsement or condoning of said behavior. Rather than face backlash for speaking up for what is right, he chose to play it safe.

One last example of people allowing their income and positions to subvert their voices was NFL players. At the height of controversy surrounding Kaepernick's kneeling during the national anthem, other players joined in. As time progressed the actions provoked wrath from fans, supporters, owners, and NFL investors all over. Soon, players who protested were getting fined, benched, traded and even blackballed from the league.

One particular incident summed the matter up totally. One Sunday, Dallas Cowboys owner Jerry Jones said publicly that any player who knelt in "disrespect" to the flag wouldn't play. The next game, none of the fifty two players dared to defy his order. Even though the act was just a symbolic gesture and didn't enact real change, the unwillingness to lose one's job for a noble cause is

[315]

just a byproduct of how money and power can negate a person's moral convictions.

Let's not get it misconstrued. The desire of one to risk their livelihoods, reputations, incomes, positions, and alliances is not an easy choice. People have families to take care of and have invested years of hard work, dedication, education and energy to enjoy the fruits of their labor. So it's easy for someone sitting on the outside looking in to voice their opinion about what someone else should do in this case. I cannot actually say what I would do if I were in any of the aforementioned positions.

However, one thing is very clear. Many times, change doesn't come without sacrifice. In 1955, the great Martin Luther King Jr. organized a bus boycott in Montgomery Alabama that lasted a year. During that time, blacks pulled together, gave up some comforts, made life difficult for themselves, and maybe even lost money, jobs, and positions. By the end of their toils however, they had brought the city to its needs and their demands had to be met.

This epic event is a blueprint of what is needed in this day and age. Everyone, both black and white, who desires to end systematic racism, and more specifically police genocide, must be willing to make a great sacrifice of personal convenience to loosen the screws and disrupt the wheels that turn this well-oiled machine of injustice.

There is no position, title, or job, too great or too small that will not have a substantial effect in this movement if leveraged properly.

In times past, many greats stood for what is right. Muhammad Ali relinquished his role as heavyweight champion, was banned from boxing, and even faced jail time for his stance on racism and war. Malcolm, Martin, Medgar and more risk their income, families, and ultimately lost their lives speaking, acting, and encouraging others to fight against racial injustices. Entertainers like Dick Gregory, Ray Charles, and others loss revenue by refusing to perform in segregated audiences. Jim Brown, Bill Russell, Kareem Abdul Jabbar, and so many more are all examples of athletes, who didn't let their fortune prohibit their inclination to fight for equality.

Since there aren't too many high profile personalities that are willing to take the risk, the impactful change must rely on the everyday layman or woman. The teacher, fireman, manager, nurse, preacher, and the like must all have the gall to put their professionality to the side when morality comes into question. Judges, police, lawyers, politicians, bankers, and businessmen must lay profit and career advancement to rest when it opposes liberty and justice for all. Everyone must open their eyes to see what and who they put in front of their obligation to the safety of humanity as a whole.

Most will agree that the change must start with those who commit egregious acts against blacks; mainly the rank and file of the law enforcement machine nationwide. This book has pointed out endless fallacies, flaws, and transgressions that have been committed against black men in the name of law and order. There is no doubt that the judicial system needs a complete overhaul in that regard.

However, the onus doesn't stop there. Every blue blooded American must examine themselves and the role they play in the hypocrisy of our democracy. So this book is most importantly a call, a beckoning to all who read to figure out what they can do to make this nation live up to the true meaning of it's creed. If not you, who? If not now, when?

Peace and Blessings

Epilogue

August, 2020

It was eleven o'clock at night. I had just left a friend's house, heading home for the evening. While riding down Elm Street, a main road in Goldsboro, NC, I spotted blue lights flashing several blocks ahead at an intersection. Figuring the police had setup one of the many roadblocks in the black part of town, I made a left.

I decided to take a shortcut on the side street heading towards the nearby project. A right at the end of this road would put me on the street I lived, Olivia Lane, only four blocks from my house. I travelled the street without a care in the world.

When I reached the stop sign, I made a right. Out of nowhere, a car also made a right behind me. Blue lights flashed as I realized that it was the police. With all of the shootings that had happened, I instantly pulled over and kept my hands on the wheel. I knew I had done nothing wrong and waited patiently for the officer to appear.

Within seconds, a black officer appeared in my side view mirror. My hands squeezed the wheels as he approached slowly. I thought about my wallet that lay on the backseat from an earlier trip to the gym. I kicked myself mentally for not having my identification within arm's reach.

"How you doing sir. Let me see your license and registration please."

As the man spoke, I noticed another white officer creeping up on the passenger side rear door. My heart thumped and my mind raced as I envisioned him opening fire when I reached for the glove compartment. I decided then not to move.

"My license is in my wallet on the backseat right there. The registration is in my glovebox but I don't want to reach for it. You can get both of them yourself," I motioned with my hands still on the wheel.

"That's okay. You can get the registration out yourself," he responded as he shone the light towards the back seat, then back to my face.

"You sure," I confirmed. "I don't want to get shot!"

"You can go ahead and get the registration out and give it to me," he ordered.

"Alright now," I said as I leaned shakily over to the passenger side. I opened the box and reached for the only piece of paper therein. I handed it to the officer and placed my right hand back on the wheel. I still kept a close eye on the other officer out of my peripheral vision. He's moved closer to the passenger door, with his hand on his gun

"Where are you coming from?" The black officer regained my attention while studying the registration.

"My friend's house," I answered.

"Where are you going?"

"I'm going home. I stay right up the street. My license is right there in my wallet. You can reach in and get if for yourself."

The officer continued to look at the registration for a few more seconds before responding.

"No, that's alright. You go ahead and get home now."

With that, he handed me the paper and walked back to his car. His words were less of suggestion and more of a command or a threat. I wasted no time in cranking my car and driving the four blocks straight to my house.

The stealth of the encounter still had me rattled. I reached the stoplight a block away, still expecting the blue lights to be spinning. They were gone; and so was the police car. They had disappeared as instantaneously as they came.

As I drove the last three blocks I thought. What was that about? Where did they come from? Why didn't he even check my license? Why did he even stop me? Are they coming back?

My mind raced for the thirty second drive. I constantly checked my mirror, expecting the police to be behind me again. They weren't. I pulled in the parking lot and let out a sigh of relief. I walked hurriedly to my apartment, turned the key, stepped in to the safety of my home and closed and locked the door securely. I sat down on the couch and thought...no man should feel like I just did, all because I saw blue lights in my rearview.

BLUE LIGHTS IN MY REARVIEW

Made in the USA
Las Vegas, NV
14 July 2025

24950491R00177